Joy Formula

joy (y)=y (God's love)^(sign of y)

Joy Formula

Inkang Kim

Joy Formula

Published by
Inscript Publishing
P.O. Box 611
Bladensburg, MD 20710-0611
www.inscriptpublishing.com

Copyright © 2018 by Inkang Kim

Cover Design by Gunwoo Kim
Cover Photo by Harin Kim

All rights reserved. No part of this publication may be used or reproduced without permission of the publisher, except for brief quotes for scholarly use, reviews or articles.

Scripture citations marked NIV are from the the Holy Bible, New International Version®, NIV® Copyright © 1973, 1978, 1984, 2011 by Biblica, Inc.® Used by permission. All rights reserved worldwide.

Library of Congress Control Number: 2018940384

ISBN: 978-0-9986690-8-3

Printed in the United States of America

To Heeryoung, Gunwoo, Harin and my parents

Table of Contents

Dedication v
Words by Friends viii
Prologue ix
Chapter 1—Would I Not be Starving? 1
Chapter 2—Before the Silence of God 8
Chapter 3—Why Do You Live? 19
Chapter 4—Perfect Plan for an Imperfect Person 27
Chapter 5—To Berkeley 42
Chapter 6—Beauty of Mathematics 55
Chapter 7—Beautiful Hidden Flowers 77
Chapter 8—Joy Formula 96
Chapter 9—God Makes Me Smile 110
Epilogue 134

Words by Friends

Bernard Picinbono (Emeritus Professor at Université d'Orsay)
Pour les français la Corée est un pays lointain dont on ne parle qu'à l'occasion des tensions politiques qui s'y manifestent. Grâce à Inkang Kim et à sa famille ce pays nous est devenu beaucoup plus proche. Nous avons admiré le courage serein et souriant rayonnant de sa personnalité qui lui a permis de se hisser au meilleur niveau de la recherche mathématique et qui trouve son origine dans une foi que nous partageons.

Françoise Dal'Bo (Professor at Université Rennes 1)
Inkang?
-Un voyageur du monde terrestre et imaginaire,
-Un homme déterminé à avancer, qui nous donne la preuve que le corps est peu de chose face à l'esprit,
-Mais surtout un précieux ami que j'ai la chance d'avoir rencontré.

Raquel Diaz (Professor at Universidad Complutense de Madrid)
Dos rasgos de la persona de Inkang Kim me impresionan hondamente: su aceptación de la vida y su fe en la vida, una combinación que le da una gran fuerza para mirar siempre hacia delante, con mucha serenidad. Todo esto queda reflejado limpiamente en este libro que nos ofrece.

Prologue

I have no memory of standing on my own legs. At the age of two, I got polio and could not walk anymore. I crawled on the ground by sitting on a vinyl pack of fertilizer and pulling it with one hand and pushing the ground with the other. People thought that I would be a beggar on the street, but God had a different plan.

Have you ever gazed at the stars and the moon in the dark night sky? As I grew up in the countryside, I used to lie on the straw mat in the front yard in the summer and fall asleep looking up at the Milky Way. I have a memory for special moons: the cold moon shining over the peach orchard at the beginning of the winter that I saw from my mother's back as we ran away from my drunken father; the gloomy moon hanging over the sky of Shinrim-dong during my freshman year of university; the large moon over the San Francisco Bay that I watched while singing hymns when I was weary during my years studying in Berkeley; the dreamy moon that I saw over the sand dunes of Rajasthan, India, while I was tired of my life. Now, the moon is smiling. Like a psalmist, I sing praises when I watch the stars and the moon.

> *When I consider your heavens, the work of your fingers, the moon and the stars, which you have set in place, what is mankind that you are mindful of them, human beings that you care for them? You have made them a little lower than the angels and crowned them with glory and honor (Psalm 8:3-5, NIV).*

The cold and sad moon now becomes a moon showing the providence and grace of God. Outside my office window, the sky is filled with greenness and aliveness. Several years have passed since I moved here to KIAS (Korea Institute for Advanced Study) from SNU (Seoul National University) at Kwanak Mountain. Around this time, I would have been teaching Stokes' theorem, topological space, and representation theory, with my hands dirty with white chalk.

The past fifty years seem like a moment: my childhood with illness and loneliness; my youth with poverty and lostness; my university years spent astray without knowing where to go and what to do, and my Berkeley years like a desert. Before I became a professor at KAIST (Korea Advanced Institute for Science and Technology) and SNU, so many things happened. Among these stories, I cannot skip the one about God who always watched over me at every corner of my life, who made me smile when I lost my smile under the heavy weight of my life, and who clothed me with joy.

From now on, I want to tell the story about God, a topologist who encountered Him, and the joy formula that he discovered.

September 12, 2017

1

Would I Not be Starving?

There once was a child living every day expecting tomorrow to be different from today.

(Gloria Vanderbilt, *Fairy Tale*)

Lost two legs

In my childhood, as I could not walk, I was staying alone in a remote village where there was no hospital, no school, and no electricity. When my parents went to the peach orchard and my brothers and sisters went to school, I lay in the room alone. Whether I played by myself, fell asleep, or woke up alone, the silence was all around. I can still feel the quietness, as if I went through a long, dark tunnel. Even at the age of three, I had to learn what solitude was and how to deal with it.

My friends were little chickens, puppies, bees, butterflies in the spring, and the nameless flowers scattered around in the backyard. I remember the warmth of spring sunshine on my cheeks, the heat haze shimmering into the air like an ephemeral hope, the pinky-peach flowers blooming in the orchard, the yellow and purple irises, the grapevine by the well, the skylark's song soaring over the barley field, the smell of acacia in May, the swaying of cosmos flowers on the road. Oh, I still remember them vividly. Maybe that's all my memories of my childhood.

In the summer of 1968, I vomited up red tomato while toddling around in a pair of red boots. For several days, I was delirious with

Last photo of the author standing with brothers and a sister at a peach orchard in 1967

high fever, and my body was so swollen that my mother took me to a hospital in the village. The doctor's diagnosis was a cold with indigestion. After two weeks, the fever was gone, but I could not walk anymore. My mother took me to the hospital again, but it was too late.

My first memory, from the bottom of my consciousness, is of looking at the sunset while lying on my mother's knees. My mother took me to every famous hospital and acupuncturist. When I was around five or six, one of my aunts recommended a famous American doctor in Sooncheon city. With hope, my mother took me there. However, the doctor said it was too late, and nothing could be done. My mother was crying in pain and left the doctor's room with me on her back. I was crying as well, resting my head against her lean back.

Through the windows of the train back home, I could see the sun setting slowly over the mountains. I looked blankly at the dusk in the darkening sky. I instinctively felt that I would have heartache throughout my life like the sunset in the dusking sky. Even now my heart is wet with sorrow whenever I see the sunset.

Once, we went to a hospital in Seoul on my cousin's recommendation. The express bus was so crowded, the motion sickness and the stench of people made us throw up. But I was watching the crowded rest area: the old hunchbacked ladies selling chewing gum, the street vendors with wooden boxes hanging around their necks stepping into the bus at the rest stops. I knew that the journey of life would not be easy for them, nor for me.

Staying at a house where my cousin worked as a maid, my mother and I went to the hospital every day. However, the doctor said that rehabilitation was the only way, but we could not afford it. Once again, my mother returned home carrying me on her back. My parents set up a chin-up bar at the corner of the front yard so I could practice walking.

Nonsan-gun Yeonmu-up Majeon-ri; that was the address of my home. My house was built away from the village road, around the corner from the peach orchard. The only visitors we had were a woman selling fish from Ganggyeong city, and a postman.

On their every visit, my mother talked with them, worrying about me.

"Will he survive without starving? What shall he do after I die?"

People thought that I could not follow the conversation at such a young age, but those words penetrated my soul like a sword. I was deeply disturbed and had bad dreams at night. I cannot remember them exactly, but I once woke up in the middle of the night while dreaming about falling into a dark, spiral abyss. I trembled at the white shine of the moon poking through the door.

Expel him, bury him

My mother sat me under the peach trees while she worked in the field. From time to time she smiled at me, lifting her tired sun-tanned face and straightening up from a weeding hoe. I was thinking about the people and the villages over the distant mountain.

The chickens and puppies were around me. They were my only friends. Each one had a unique character: wild one, weak one, cowardly one, greedy one, wily one. I named one of chickens *kiker*, which means tall. I could understand their language. When a cock seduces a hen, he uses a low baritone tone, "Togdog tok tok, togdog tok tok." When there is a danger like a lurking weasel nearby, they scream out "Kogog, kogog," while straightening their necks and tails. I used to call out the chickens with the sound, "Ko ko ko" when I had a bug for them to eat. They regarded me as one of theirs. But when someone's birthday came, my mother slaughtered one of the chickens. I could not eat it because it had been my friend.

There were tons of work to be done in the orchard and the field. Starting in early spring, the peach trees were pruned, and then strawberries were planted. During the summer, my family worked until late night picking peaches and sorting them into boxes. Though my father never went to school, he was able to count the number of boxes and their exact price. It was past midnight when my family finally loaded the peach boxes into a truck from Seoul. After the peaches, they picked the tobacco leaves, dried them in the vinyl house, and finally packed them up into small dumps.

They also grew rice, sesame, beans, potatoes, and sweet potatoes in the field.

Throughout the year, there was not a single day that they were off work.

I used to watch them, half-sleeping, working diligently under the dim oil lamp. I fell asleep to the lullaby of twinkling stars in the summer sky, smelling the smoke of the mosquito-repelling fire lit in the corner of the house.

My mother prepared the rice sake and kimchi for morning break. At lunchtime, she set a fire to make lunch for the workers in the scorching sun with her face full-flushed. To help my busy mom, I sat in front of the burning logs to keep them burning. My whole body and face were also burning in the sizzling heat of summer. The workers filled their stomachs with rice, taken from a pan with their dirty hands. Some women brought their children to lunch, but my mother was generous and fed them all.

After lunch, workers had a nap for thirty minutes. The summer's midday sun, which made people squint even by looking at it, melted down the souls of the workers covered with sweat and dirt. They slept well with their faces covered with towels and straw-hats.

At the evening sunset, when the heat was calming down, the workers returned home. My family had a late dinner after my parents, sisters and brothers, who came back from school, finished up the last of the work. Even after the whole family was in bed snoring, my mother could not rest. Only when she finished laundry, washed the dishes, and prepared the next day's meal, could she go to bed around dawn.

Yet the heavy labor had been lighter than what my father's violence inflicted. His bad drinking habit wreaked an unforgivable scar on my family. Whenever we heard my father's footsteps after he was drinking late, we felt a terrible fear. When he threw up the dinner table and started to wield his fists, my brothers and sisters ran away. My mother or sister took me on their back to run away as well. When there was no time to take me with them, I stayed there alone trembling with fear of death.

My father harassed my mom, "Expel Inkang away. Bury him

underground now!"

After the long night of war, my mom used to hug me tight on her knees.

"I must live to protect you...."

Since then, I have buried deep inside my heart the caress of my mom's rough hands on my hair.

With brothers and a sister when the author was a baby, around 1969

We cannot admit a child like him

My childhood passed by even though it seemed halted there forever. My nine-year-old sister entered elementary school late hoping that she could go to school together with me. However, the school was too far away for her to carry me on her back, and the school did not allow it, either. When I was seven, my mother took me to school, but the principal did not accept me after he saw that I could not walk, saying, "It is impossible to accept him since his disability is so serious. We cannot admit him."

It was my first official rejection from society.

How much I cried in my heart on the way back home on such a windy spring day!

My mother said to me, "My little baby, are you cold?"

She put my freezing feet in her pockets. What else could she say? How can I estimate the depth of despair that my mother was in when there was nothing she could do for her child except warming his feet?

In the end, I stayed home until I turned eleven. Not one to be bored, I did the chores. I packed the dried tobacco leaves, sorted beans for bean sprouts, and made the fire for meals. I learned how to read and write over the shoulders of my brothers and sisters, and I managed to learn math by reading my sister's textbook. I did my sister's math, art, and writing homework and other projects since she was busy with housework. I learned to sing while listening to Nam Jin and Nahoona, famous Korean singers, on the radio. I was able to memorize entire songs by listening to them a few times just after they came out, amazing my sisters. I recited the English words while my sister at middle school was studying English.

When I was home alone during the daytime, I read all my brothers and sisters' books: the novels of André Gide; "The Last Leaf" by O. Henry; short stories of Korean authors from 1940 to 1970. The novel "Le Petit Prince" by Saint-Exupéry, borrowed from a cousin, impressed the loneliest boy in the world a lot.

Even though I did not fully understand the novel, I dreamed about traveling from country to country like the little prince traveled from star to star. But the only world to which I was allowed to go was my shabby house, the peach orchard, and the rice field.

Six children together around 1973

2

Before the Silence of God

With respect to the theological view of the question; this is always painful to me. — I am bewildered— I had no intention to write atheistically. But I own that I cannot see, as plainly as others do...

There seems to me too much misery in the world. I cannot persuade myself that a beneficent and omnipotent God would have designedly created the Ichneumonidae with the express intention of their feeding within the living bodies of caterpillars, or that a cat should play with mice. Not believing this, I see no necessity in the belief that the eye was expressly designed.

-In the letter of Charles Darwin to Asa Gray

To a rehabilitation center

In my small village, there lived a blind person. He sold chewing gum and some snacks for children from his own small room. After he groped for the money he received, he handed out the item. But the little rascals in the village very often stole many things from him. It made me gloomy. If I were selling products like him, I would just have to watch the thieves run away from me since I could not chase after them. If I cannot sell products like him, what kind of things could I do to support myself in the future?

Since my mother was not educated, she sent the children to school so they wouldn't regret missing out later.

But my father was not happy. "It is useless to send them to school. Make them work at home. To make money, one has to do business!"

He beat my mother when she gave her own hard-earned money to children for school tuition. But my second sister finally did something extraordinary. She was accepted to a women's high school in Daejon after she ran away from home with a sack of rice. Right after she graduated, she called her brothers to Daejon for their education. One day, she called me at home.

"I heard on a radio about a school where children like you can study. Even you can learn some job skills at a boarding school."

It was the Sungsae Rehabilitation School that my mother took me to. I clenched my teeth so I wouldn't cry when my mother and sister took me there and left. I wished I could follow them back home, despite my drunken father being there. Still, I knew what had to be done. If I didn't want to be a street beggar, I needed to study here and learn the skill of woodcarving and printing.

As she left, my mother kept looking back again and again. I tried to smile, holding back tears. I waved my hands. "Mom, I am okay. I can do it."

I was eleven years old.

The first fight

Even before the fear of a new environment managed to set in, sorrow and nervousness came upon me. After the departure of my mother, a guy next to me picked a fight.

"Yo, you want to fight? To see who is stronger?"

For the first time, I fought a fight without any reason. It was customary there to pick a fight to order the ranks. He gave me a bloody nose, and I became his henchman.

The food there was terrible. I had never eaten such salty kimchi in my life!

I guess that was the only way to provide a hundred students with proper food. Looking at the other children gulping down food with salty kimchi and dried radish, I couldn't finish the meal and sneaked out. I cried at the building corner. Eventually, I wrote a letter to my mother asking her to take me back home, but I could not post it. I knew that I had to endure if this was the road that I was to take. Unlike myself, there were many abandoned children. Even though they had parents, if their parents do not come anymore to pick them up, the children are considered abandoned.

"My mother will come back to pick me up," I comforted myself.

At the entrance of the rehab center, I took a level test for reading, addition, subtraction, and multiplication. I was assigned to the third grade. I wound up placing first in the first exam, which I was not prepared for. For this reason, a classmate, Enyoung, did not like me. Enyoung was from Seoul and was always in first place before I came here. She even spurred water from her mouth on me after she drank a cup of water. It had never happened to me before.

"I hate you really," she told me.

Even though I was beaten badly my first fight, I did better in subsequent fights. Some kids teased me by calling me "chicken girl" due to my shy character, but when I was determined, my fists were strong. Sometimes, even a fight is a good thing. It gave me the courage to fight against things that are unjust.

I helped the other children with math and fractions after school. They did not bother me anymore. Since I was good at calculation, I also helped out in the snack shop, a small one selling chewing gum, snacks and bread. I also wrote addresses on the envelopes sent out to the students' parents.

One of my friends, Jeonwha, had shriveled hands. He wrote with a pencil pinched between his chin and shoulder. "I am going to go out looking for my parents when I become an adult," he once told me.

He was a good guy. He never showed any resentment towards his parents. I prayed when Jeonwha met his parents, they would feel the same way.

Life there was like being in an army. We worked hard in groups to clean up after meals and before bed, as dictated by the strong brothers and their fists. About six people slept in each room. Starting with the strongest brother, everyone took their favorite spot in the room. Older guys sometimes went out to drink, avoiding the superintendent. If they were caught, they were beaten practically to death. I could not understand such harsh punishment. Rules and punishments were more abundant than understanding and kindness.

There were many lice in the dorms, especially during the winter. A few times a month, my second sister took me to her place to wash me, do laundry, and cook a bean-sprout dish for me. While she could have been spending her time on self-development and leisure, she sacrificed herself and her time for her brothers. She gave up every Sunday to do my laundry and wash me.

White funeral car

There was a chamber group called "Bethesda," made up of several guys in wheelchairs who had graduated from the Sungsae Rehab Center. It consisted of violins, a cello, and a viola, and it is fairly well-known. They came to the center to teach the children for free.

I wanted to learn how to play the violin, but I could not afford the instrument. There was an older boy who learned the violin, but he died a few years later of necrotizing fasciitis. It was a sad experience. The rehab center was a small duplicate of birth, death, and agony; broken, moaning souls ranging from ten to thirty years old, stricken with various disabilities and living in the shadow of the world. Many children were abandoned there since their parents could not take care of them.

Sometimes, churches and NGOs visited us to distribute bread and milk. Particularly around Christmas, many churches performed concerts and plays for us. After their visit, we only felt more deserted. If some organization visited us, the place was crowded with children hoping to have their portion. However, only one visit event made us more miserable. Helping and comforting someone is only possible through a long-term relationship. Even the holiest and religious act can deepen the isolation if it does not develop into a relationship. Helping others is not a temporary, shallow, emotional thing. It is only possible through a genuine sharing of one's life.

Some of us died from lingering diseases, since we were cast out and crippled. On those days, a small funeral car came to pick up the corpses. There was no one to greet them for the last time, not even their parents. On those days, I went up to the river bank and gazed into the sky all day long. The children were abandoned even by their parents because of their disabilities. Oh! How much innocent blood should be shed for this world to be pardoned? I could not suppress the anger inside of me when I looked at my dying friends, cast out by their family and society at such a young age. I felt the same anger as Camus, described in a book regarding him. "Je n'étais pas négateur du ciel, ni négateur de Dieu, mais simplement homme qui accuse le ciel de se taire, de ne pas répondre à la douleur des hommes."

A pastor came every week to deliver a sermon. Service was mandatory. I was not convinced when he said that God loves us. I had perfect scores in everything but Bible class.

Standing upright

Even though I got to know the bitterness of life at such an early age, I was not always gloomy. At the rehab center, we exchanged jokes, did silly things, sang pop songs, and played sports together. Even though we could not use our legs, we played soccer and baseball using our hands, and we raced by supporting our legs with our hands. We tumbled around in the playground. We crawled on the ground laughing and screaming. Some people watching us playing this way were skeptical, or became sad and shed tears. But this

made others think about their lives again. A violinist who came to Yousung for the hot spring saw children playing and crawling on the ground. It shocked her tremendously, but she came back to teach children violin for free. That was the origin of the chamber group Bethesda.

After ten years of sedentary life, all the muscles of my legs were shrunk and could not stretch out. Once a week, I went through a rehab treatment. This was tremendous torture for me. They put hot packs on my legs for twenty minutes until the flesh became red. Once I was ready, one therapist held my arms while the other started to straighten my legs pitilessly. I cried out in pain and screamed, spat, and even bit the therapists. They straightened my legs so I could wear braces to walk with crutches. It took me two years. Often, it takes pain and endurance to cure hardened bone or a numbed heart.

In the sixth grade, I could stand straight with braces and crutches. At last, I could see others at eye level. The joy was short-lived. My hips and back hurt too much. Rashes developed on my knees, and my hands had blisters. Since I supported my body weight on my crutches' armpit supporters, I had bruises on my armpits. It was extreme pain. Some children could not bear it, and they went back to wheelchairs. But I endured. I could not go back to my previous state. The rehab center trained us to walk along the riverbank, about two kilometers, until the crutches became a part of our body. Finally, I became a *Homo erectus*. As a reward for enduring pain, the crutches offered me the liberty to walk toward the world.

Meeting a teacher

It was the greatest blessing in my life that I met a teacher, Choi Hwabok, with tiger eyebrows. He voluntarily transferred from a normal school to teach children with disabilities. He was my teacher when I was in sixth grade. He combed his hair in a neat pomade and wore a proper suit. I skipped from fourth to sixth grade at his recommendation.

"Hey guys, his eyebrows are raised. Watch out!"

He scolded us whenever we were rude or acted improperly. There was no excuse, even for disabled children. Still, he never beat us. If we did not understand something in class, he repeated it ten times.

"Now, relax and open your mouth wide."

He taught us how to sing while he played the organ. Even the child with a speaking disability sang well enough during singing class. He also conducted an orchestra, where I played the harmonica.

Our orchestra won first prize in a national competition held at the Samyouk Rehab Center. He taught me calligraphy, and I won a prime minister's prize in a calligraphy competition.

My teacher was famous while working at a normal school. It was known that if he trains a student, then that student will be able to enter a prominent school. However, he was happier teaching at a rehab center than working in a public school just to teach the entrance exam.

He would say, "Everyone is good at at least one thing. Let's try to find out what."

He gave us hope when we had no promising future. He told me that I was good at studying. "Inkang, you must enter a normal middle school and pursue your studies to the end."

He gave me sample exams used in ordinary public schools and even some books from Gyohaksa. He erased important words in a history book so we would memorize the book from beginning to end.

As graduation approached, my sister told me to stay at the rehab center to learn some practical skills. It was obvious that it would be difficult for me to get a job, even if I graduated from university. But my teacher persuaded her that I must continue studying. "No one knows the future. Inkang must pursue his studies," my teacher said.

He wanted to send me to Daejon Middle School and visited the school several times by bike to ask for my admission. But the school was not convinced. He drew a map from our rented house to the school to show that it was short enough for me to walk. Still, the school did not believe him. "There are too many stairs in the school. We cannot accept him."

Finally, he threatened the principal. "You will regret it if you do not accept him. He will make your school famous!"

Maybe it did work. I was admitted to the school!

Probably, he did not know how many great things he did for me in my life. Fifteen years later, when I became a professor at KAIST, I visited him. He had gray hair but was still at the rehab center, teaching disabled children. He had heard rumors about me, and he was so happy that I became a professor at a university. He asked me to give a speech to the children. I did not know what to say, and I knew too well that they needed neither cheap comfort nor advice.

I told them, "Do not compare your life to others', whatever life is given to you. No one can live your life for you. You must live it out. You cannot throw it away, nor think it too light. Our life is holy and precious."

My teacher and I had lunch together in a hilly restaurant selling oak tofu. During lunch, he told me, "I knew the road that you must take when you solved the problems, that you never learned, about the eclipse and the zodiac. Isn't that a teacher who can read his student's ability?"

I could not sufficiently express my gratitude for his unconditional love for me. The only way to pay him back would be by taking care of the soul and life of my students, as he did for me.

When I got married, he came with Jeonwha to Changwon to celebrate. When my son was born, I asked him to name my child. He named both my children. He retired happily from Sungsae Rehab School and is now teaching Chinese at Korea-Chinese-Center.

The teacher stood me up and opened up a road for a boy with polio who could not dream, who didn't even know whether he could dream. He is the best teacher that I respect the most.

Back home

I moved out of the rehab center and into ordinary middle school. Most of my friends stayed at the center to learn carving and printing skills. The products, such as wooden dolls, souvenirs, and printed materials, are not competitive enough in the market. They worked all day long, but it didn't help much for their living. But there was no alternative.

The founder of the rehab center was a medical doctor. People abandoned their children with disabilities in front of the hospital, so he made his house into a rehab center for them. He was a Christian. Around that time, people got polio by the thousands every year. The year I got polio, 1968, many other children got polio also. The rehab center became known throughout the country, and a hundred children came. That was the time when parents hid their disabled children at home. My father also was ashamed of taking me out to the village.

According to my own experiences, rehabilitation should take place in the middle of society. The disabled should not be secluded by collecting them together. Learning how to accept differences and living together with ordinary people is genuine rehabilitation. Learning a few job skills in sequestered conditions cannot teach people how to live together and how to be cooperative in society. A disability is not a cross for just a disabled person and their family to bear. Society at large must bear the burden. Disabled people should go to regular schools. Even if they come home crying because their peers make fun of them, they should not give up. If the disabled are secluded, society would not know that they exist. They should not hide; people should see them in normal situations.

I will never forget my experience at the rehab center and I relish the memories of my friends and our time together: Changduk, who stammered and wore his father's old shoes; Jeonwha, who was determined to find his parents; Enyoung, who hated me; Mangi, who was a classmate in sixth grade and is now running a jewelry store at Daejon; Younsoo, who had the same disability as I; Youtae, who sang the music of Song Chang-sik very well. I fondly remember those boys and girls chatting and laughing under the fragrant ivy trees, those friends with both physical and mental disabilities, those boys who could not even move their fingers and had to lie down all day long.

I got to know the valley of death and shadow of the land. Three years of experience in the rehab center helped me fully understand who I am and where I was. That was the desert of my life, without hope, promise, or comfort. I could not accept God, who did not answer the questions in my young mind, and who was seemingly silent to those of us who suffered without reason. Despite this, He must have trained me. This life desert would become a land of conversion and promise if I turned my eyes away from the land, where hope is dried out, and towards the sky.

I cannot remember the day of graduation clearly. I gave a farewell speech, I guess. But I cannot even remember who came, which awards I got, or what we ate after the ceremony. I was just happy about going back home.

In peach orchard before departing for the rehab center in 1976

3

Why Do You Live?

Without candlelight, without thinking of any miracle
I stepped forward to a dark altar
I was cold and poor. To rub my frozen hands
I even could not gather my hands to pray
How long was I rubbing my hands?
At that moment, a candle was lit in my hands...
(Song Chanho, *Candle Light*)

Henchman friends

During the entrance ceremony for Daejon Middle School, a tall, handsome guy pledged in as our representative. He scored first place in the placement test. In the first test, boys from private elementary schools did well. They carried a bag full of all kinds of supplementary books that I never heard of, five or six books for each subject. They practiced the same problems over and over and tried to solve really difficult weird problems. It seemed like a waste of time to me. I could figure out the important things in the textbook and predict what kind of problems would be on the exam. Knowing too many things does not help all the time. One has to memorize things logically. Since nobody taught me how to solve problems, that helped me a lot. Since I struggled by myself to figure out the problem, I never forgot the solution. I did not study that hard, but I got better as time went by.

After school, I played with my friends at home, in the two rooms we rented for a cheap price. The room was located uphill in the town. My sister worked, and my brothers were in high school. When it rained, I was drenched because I could not use an umbrella. When it snowed, I slipped while walking down the hill with my crutches. I had to walk about thirty minutes to go to school. I could not carry my bag, but thankfully some of the guys carried it for me. Those guys were from humble families, and they did not do well in studies, either. There were called henchmen, or in modern terminology, losers. Some of them delivered newspapers in the morning, and they often didn't do their homework or concentrate in class. Teachers always picked them for punishment, but nonetheless, they were pure in heart. We gathered at my house, sang together loudly with a guitar, and had ramen together. I liked playing with them until I was exhausted. Then, I taught them and helped them with their homework.

Often, during exams, they asked me for answers to questions. One of them was Dukhee, who really hated studying but was pretty good at fighting. I watched them fighting often. Each class had about sixty students, 720 boys each grade, about 2000 boys total. It was an all-boys school, which is like a minefield where a sudden explosion could happen at any moment.

After school, at the corner of the baseball field, the students staged a fighting event, called "today's battle," held almost every day. There were rules for fair fighting: never use stones; never scatter sand at the eyes; never kick in the crotch. Everyone circled around the two fighters. I became a referee. They thought I was fair. If one fighter's nose started bleeding, the fight was usually over.

Later, Dukhee studied the drum at Chungnam University. Now, he teaches students music and runs a musical instrument shop. Teacher Choi was right; everyone is good at something. Most of my friends went to technical high school after middle school. The guy who delivered newspapers still threw one at my house for three years after we had parted. I really appreciated his friendship whenever I picked up the newspaper from the snow-covered winter ground. They still call me from time to time. How happy we were together at the middle school!

Why do you live?

The adolescent boys gathered in groups and mimicked adults. Some groups were into meeting girls; other groups roamed around the city smoking and drinking. They went through the stormy days carnally, but I went through the unstable days mentally. I tried in vain to resolve the suffocating emotion and chaos of adolescence by playing guitar, writing novels and poems, reflecting and reading.

My wandering got worse in senior year. I detoured from a street with tall trees on the way back home after school. I pondered heavy questions in life, ones too difficult for a teenage boy to answer, and I arrived home after the street lights were already on. Maybe I did not want to enter a house where no one was waiting.

Around that time, I was into the work of Franz Kafka. I could not completely understand his novels, but the idea of a human feeling like a cog in the machine of modern society, or a human being turning into a worm in a distorted structure, seemed really sad. From reading "The Dwarf Launches a Little Ball" by Jo Sehee and "Death of a Salesman" by Arthur Miller, I could see the self-contradictory and dark side of modern society. I was also into the works of Albert Camus. He vividly depicted the status of mankind who wants to go somewhere, who tries to escape the surrounding darkness, but does not know where we are from or where we are going. He failed to suggest a salvation, but he represented my mind by saying that humanity cannot be the superman (Übermensch) that Nietzsche described, but is just lost at the crossroads. Sometimes I pondered on this for hours sitting in the rain on a small hill behind the house or sitting in the dark of my room.

My expression was getting darker. The teacher in charge of my class spoke to me as he was passing by. "My mental age seems to be the same as yours. But Inkang, shouldn't we be happy?"

One day, he called a counselor for me. The counselor took me to a remote place and gave me a bunch of good advice. She thought my problem was due to adolescence and frustration from my disability. It was kind of a long sermon. A lethargic afternoon sunlight passed through the window onto the floor in the silence. I asked her quietly, "Do you know why we live?"

"..."

She couldn't answer.

"If you do not know why we live, then why do you live?"

She was disconcerted by this punching question asked by a middle school boy.

"Well... To be honest, I do not know."

Our conversation stopped there. She told the teacher that I was out of her capacity. I feel sorry for her now, but frankly, I just asked the question that I was struggling with at that time.

Luckily, God did not let go of me. Up the hill from the house, there was a small church. I could not remember why I went there. I asked Jeondosa every day about God and belief. Why we live, for what we live, and how we know God exists. Jeondosa thought I was a difficult guy for raising philosophical questions. Most middle school students came to the church for dating. I could not bear such a light atmosphere. Even though I stopped going to church, surely I took a step of faith rather than being Übermensch. That was my first attempt to encounter God.

Perfect score in entrance exam

Throughout the three years of middle school, I was assigned a class located on the ground floor because, unfortunately, there was no elevator in the school. During PE, I was left alone in the room. Sometimes I wrote, or I walked around watching students play soccer and baseball. When the acacia bloomed, I wrote poems and short stories while sitting on the bench. Meditation, study, reading, writing, and playing guitar filled up most of my day. Teachers were kind to me since I was good at studying, drawing, and music.

Still, I remember an old English teacher from the first year of middle school. She gave us a quiz every day. I got perfect scores throughout the semester, and she complimented me on it. Maybe compliments are the best way to educate students, since I still remember the compliment thirty years later.

I was pretty good at studying and was always one of the top five students in school. I scored first place on the high school entrance practice test. Some of the students with high grades at the beginning of middle school did not do so well as time went by. They took separate lessons, either by private tutors or group study. Daechi-dong private lessons are quite famous in Korea. Still, the kids with private lessons lost their competitiveness later. Those kids, forced by their parents to study, lost their momentum eventually or wandered off when they lost confidence in what they were doing. That is the hardship of the long run. To overcome it, one has to set up their own goals for study. I studied hard so I would not be a burden on my parents and the society I belonged to, and also that I would have a better life than my parents.

In 1981, the day before the high school entrance exam, my teacher touched my shoulder, encouraging me. "The fame of Daejon Middle School is upon your shoulders!"

On exam day, I was calm. Apart from a few problems in the art subject, the exam was not difficult. I analyzed it logically, as I did to solve any problem. After the exam, the teacher asked me to write down the answers I put in the exam. He graded it. His voice was shaking when he said, "Inkang, perfect score!"

My classmates clapped and howled.

After the official results were released, reporters came from Daejon's broadcasting media and newspapers. I was interviewed for the first time in the school's main office. They asked how I prepared for the exam. My answer was, "I studied normally using the school's textbooks and instructions. I slept sufficiently." Maybe that's a lie for many people, but that was the truth for me. I could not afford any extra private lessons, nor supplementary books, and I slept a lot since I was weak.

The next day, on my way to school, a woman from next door greeted me by saying, "Student, I saw you on TV last night. You got a perfect score!"

I smiled back. We didn't have a TV, and I didn't get to see myself on TV. But before graduation, the school took a picture of me. The principal told me that my photo would be among those that glorified the school.

Era before a storm

I was assigned to Chungnam High School. My siblings and I moved near the school, to Youchen-dong. My mother needed a spine operation and could not work anymore in the orchard. My family sold the orchard at a cheap price and joined us in Daejon. It was the first time in a long time that my entire family was together, but the situation was not good. There was no regular income, but there were three university students and one high schooler in the family. We had to earn our own tuition. I got a fellowship from the city. Since I entered the school at first place, I was exempt from paying tuition.

My father carried my bag now. He brought it to school when he went out to work early in the morning, and he took it back when he returned home. There was not much work for him since he had no skills. Every day he went to a construction site, or swept the street, or did weed pulling organized by a local municipal office. He was still drinking heavily.

"Will there be peace today?"

We all felt restless whenever he returned home. I know how a family's instability can destroy the soul of people. We suffered from the mental agony caused by disharmony with my father, much worse than economic poverty. He did not get along well with my cousin's family living in an extra house next door. My oldest brother kept out of the house, residing in some student's home as a private tutor. I tried to understand my father. How much I had wanted to come back to the house when I was at the rehab center!

But finally, alcohol took him down. One day, he collapsed, vomiting blood from a hole in his stomach. But my mother took care of him earnestly, and he recovered quickly. Afterward, he quit smoking for his health. My mother's love towards her husband surpassed even her children's understanding, even though my father abused, beat, and maltreated her throughout their lives. My second sister moved out when she got married to a good man, though belatedly since she took care of her brothers. Even after marriage, she cared for her father and brothers when my mother moved to Seoul with me for university. I was always sorry for my sister's sacrifice. I bow to her for her sacrifice since she never complained about her family, nor refused the burden of family imposed on her. Rather, she took the cross willingly.

I never had my own room. My place was at the corner of the main room, where my parents watched TV loudly. Even though I entered the school at first place, I didn't care much about the teacher's expectations for me. To pass the time, I read English novels like "The Great Gatsby" by F. Scott Fitzgerald, and "The Old Man and the Sea" by Ernest Hemingway.

I watched American Forces Korea Network on the old TV set, which I had to hit from time to time to make operate. I watched "weekend movies" on TV, which spurred my curiosity about different lives and lands that I had never visited. While the other students stayed at school late to study, I came home early and studied or played alone. I had a very independent character. If somebody forced me to study, probably I wouldn't do it. God is perfect!

Still, I had always been among the top two students in high school. I was usually quiet and speculative, but deep inside I had another, more rebellious and non-compromising character. When we had a chemistry exam, I was suspicious about the corrected answer to one problem. I thought about the problem again, and I was sure that my answer was correct. I talked to the chemistry teacher. He seemed to ignore me at first, but I insisted. Finally, he accepted that my solution was correct. However, he tried to correct just my score since the whole school was already graded.

"That is not fair," I complained. "You should correct all the students' exams. What is correct is correct."

He seemed upset and angry, but finally, he corrected all the students' exams. Looking back on it now, I feel ashamed since the teacher accepted his error and corrected the entire school's papers, yet I behaved like a rude, self-righteous knight.

My high school life was like the day before a great storm. I suppressed many questions about life and suffocating emotions for the sake of entering a university. Since my family situation was going nowhere, the best thing I could do was to go to a university with a fellowship. After university, I wanted to take care of my parents. For such a bright future, I had to postpone my philosophical questions. I committed myself to study.

4

Perfect Plan for an Imperfect Person

God moves in a mysterious way
His wonders to perform;
He plants His footsteps in the sea
And rides upon the storm.
Deep in unfathomable mines
Of never failing skill
He treasures up His bright designs
And works His sov'reign will.
(William Cowper,
God Moves in a Mysterious Way)

Choosing Mathematics

I didn't do very well on the university entrance exam. The test was on the third floor, and the restroom was outside the building. There was not enough time for me to go to the restroom, and I had to hold the pee until the end. These days, a disabled student can take a test on the first floor in the caring room, but at that time, there was no such arrangement for me. Nevertheless, I got a high enough score to be able to enter Seoul National University.

My high school teacher recommended mathematics, saying to me, "Inkang, since you are very good at math, how about applying to the math department at Seoul National University?"

Considering my immobility, it was a good idea. First, I had to avoid subjects requiring physical prowess, such as medicine and engineering. Second, literature, especially the law; even if I passed the bar exam, it is difficult for a disabled person to be appointed as a judge. That was the reality in Korea. *Isn't it enough that a judge has a sound head, heart, and hands?* Third, I had to avoid subjects requiring experiments, such as biology and chemistry.

My father was against me going to Seoul because we didn't have the money, but my brothers and sisters encouraged me. "You should move higher than here."

My brother bought the application form and submitted it. A few months later, I went to the interview. The professors were worried about my physical condition.

"There are many stairs in the school. Can you manage it?"

"I don't know, but I will give it a try."

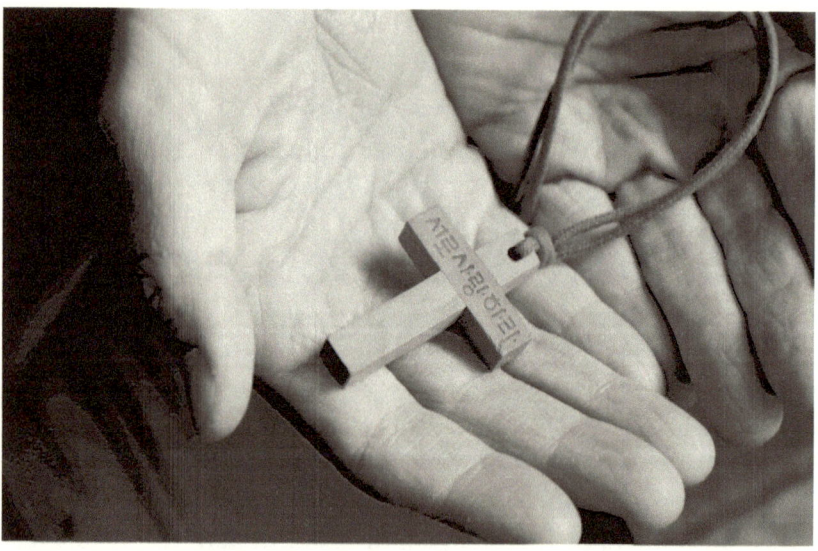

Their response was not bad. Furthermore, it turned out that I have red-green color-blindness. Finally, I was admitted to the math department. My mother and I moved to Seoul with only two thousand dollars. We rented a room in Shinrim-dong in the basement of my high school mate's house. Originally designed as a car garage, the place had been transformed into a room with no windows and no sunlight.

Luckily, the tuition was exempted with a full scholarship and some stipend meant for only one person in the department. Since there were two of us, I taught a high schooler to get some extra money.

Now, university life had begun. It was not difficult to follow the lessons, but the problem was moving around the classes. If other students needed five minutes to go from one place to another, I needed fifteen minutes, thirty minutes if there were stairs. If a class was on the fourth floor in the literature department and the next class on the fourth floor in the natural science department, the lesson was over while I was still moving.

One day, an event occurred and stuck in my mind. It was the beginning of the semester. I had to move to the next class, but no one could help me with my heavy bag. I asked someone next to me, "Can you help me with my bag?"

Usually, an ordinary student would kindly help me, but this student was different.

"You have to do it yourself!"

My face blushed, but it woke me up as terribly as if I had jumped into icy water.

Didn't I take the kindness and sacrifice of others toward me for granted, with the excuse of my handicap? Did I take advantage of them? Are those little acts of kindness like carrying my bag, or yielding seats for me—are they really small? What about the sacrifices of my parents, brothers, and sisters? Who am I to abuse pity even though I hate pity? I was greatly ashamed.

I bought a backpack. It was heavy, but I felt like I jumped 10 meters in the air. Afterward, I always tried to solve problems by myself if I could. There are so many things I can do by myself that I never imagined I could before. Warm love helps a person stand up, but cold critique makes the person move forward.

A certain smile

Once I was admitted to a university, those philosophical conundrums I had postponed before started to torture me. From the beginning of university, I had already lost much hope in life when I realized I had to take care of myself, even financially, contrary to high school life, when I could just dedicate my time to study.

"Why did I struggle so much to attend this university?"

We have a hundred years on earth, at maximum. If there is no clear reason to live, why am I suffering to live? I isolated myself from ordinary university life, like drinking, group trips, and dating. The Roman philosopher Seneca's words comforted me. "No matter how painful life is, that life is short is our hope."

Day to day, I sustained myself by depending on this pessimistic saying. But God had a different plan for me.

It was an autumn day when it happened. The leaves were changing colors. I was alone, walking back home after finishing the day, when it started to rain. Because I could not hold an umbrella, I had no choice but to keep walking in the rain. Then, someone stepped in to share her umbrella with me. But the umbrella was too small, and now both of us were getting wet. I told her, "Since I am already wet, you can go by yourself."

Maybe I wanted to say that there was no hope left for me, that I had given up on myself. But she insisted on sharing the umbrella. When we were exiting the gate of the university, she asked me if I ever thought about God. I answered her aggressively, "Maybe a hundred times or a thousand times more than you!"

That was not a lie. How many times did I ask God, about my raison d'être and purpose of my life?

She walked me to my house and introduced me to ESF (Evangelical Students Fellowship). She encouraged me to participate in a Bible study group on campus.

Later, while I was reading on the grass before class, someone from another campus ministry team suggested a one-on-one Bible study to learn about God. I decided to read the Bible seriously. In one-on-one Bible study, we read Genesis, and with the ESF people, we studied John together in an empty classroom in the literature department. The brothers and sisters in the group asked me if I entered university late because I looked old. Maybe my face was gray and gloomy, as if volcanic ashes covered my face. My difficult life already made me look old. Upon reading the gospel of John, I started to get to know Jesus, who came as a light into this world, whose words were incarnated into flesh, who is the Logos of the universe.

Someday in that winter, I was reading a book in a library. It

ESF Winter retreat in 1989

was about a nurse, over forty years old, who took care of miners. One stormy night, upon hearing that the mine had collapsed and several miners were buried inside, she hurriedly rode a bike to the site. She bumped into a pole and was knocked out on the road. She broke her spine, and the lower half of her body was paralyzed. Several years later, she was still taking care of the miners in her wheelchair.

Somebody asked her, "What on Earth is the source of this power?" She replied simply. "If God is watching me and smiling at me, I can do this until I die."

At that moment, I realized that even though no person was watching over me, and that I could not find a reason to live here, there was someone who was smiling at me from above. The meaning of life cannot be obtained by my efforts, but it is revealed by God from above. And only God has the answers to "why." He was waiting for me to experience the loneliness of life and learn to understand the pain of those who are lonely. Jesus is almighty, yet he limited his infiniteness to time and space. He came to us as a little baby and participated in my loneliness, staying with me throughout the struggling nights, by filling my fragile body, which will return to earth after several decades, with his infiniteness and almightiness. God allowed me such countless questions and pains so that I may learn his meekness.

It was snowing while I was walking back home, but I did not feel cold, for my heart was filled his warmth.

A shepherd

I kept reading the Bible to know God better. The students at ESF all had similar questions in life. Nowadays, churches put much effort into young adult ministry, knowing that the future depends on them; but around that time, young adult groups did not get enough attention from the churches in Korea.

Our Bible study was serious, and any questions were allowed. Diverse students came to the meeting. Some did not know about God at all and just came to study the Bible as one of the classics. Some came to know God more deeply even though they had belonged to a church for a long time. Some had family difficulties. Those with much interest in the structure of society and injustice questioned why God did not interfere with this absurd world where the innocent suffer, but evil people thrive.

Those students from the countryside, who were praised by their fellow villagers for having been accepted into Seoul National University, who had a village feast thrown in their honor and a card pitched at the entrance of the village, were depressed by their more brilliant peers and their unfamiliarity with city culture. Those students without any problems were unhappy because they did not know what happiness was. People might think that the SNU students are happy because they are brilliant and have a bright future, but that is not the case.

The chasm between their low self-esteem and their parents' high expectations, the competition, and the pressure to succeed—all these made them desolate. There is no one who does not need God's consolation. My heart was broken to see friends who suffered mentally more than I. Even though I was a poor, disabled person, I shared an embracing brother's love with them. Everyone has their own cross. God is fair.

A shepherd, Kim Hoikwon, returned from his military service to Kwanak ESF. He was converted during his university years and became a good disciple. He wore only one suit with old shoes and had moppy hair. He studied English literature as an undergraduate, then philosophy as a graduate, then theology in Jangsin seminary. That was why he was so knowledgeable about the Bible, philosophy, theology, and literature. His viewpoint was broad, from a personal life to the current history, and he was certain that the power of the Holy Spirit could change not only individual people but also the entire society.

Many students from different universities came to listen to his spiritual and intellectual sermons. Sixty square meters of the small gathering hall were filled with the enthusiasm of students. Some students even stood in the doorway. We were thirsty for the truth.

This epoch was under the regime of Chun Doo-hwan. The university was filled with chaos and tear bomb gas from a fight between the police and protesters, there were gatherings at the

ESF Summer retreat in 1989

Acropolis, and students were burning themselves to death. Even though the era was in darkness, we were born again by the gospel of God to become warriors of Jesus.

The shepherd, Kim Hoikwon, went to Princeton Seminary for his Ph.D. After that, he served as a pastor in Ilsan Dooree Church, and now he is a professor of Sungsil University, still lighting fires in the heart of young students.

I also changed slowly. During chapel service, I played gospel songs on the guitar that I used to play to soothe myself. I became a shepherd for young souls and prayed for them. I never went on excursions or senior trips, but now I went to a retreat with my sheep. Especially in the summer nationwide retreat, I learned the love of Jesus, who came to Earth in search for lost souls, who shed his blood and tore his body on the cross to reconcile us with God.

I still remember two students I took care of. One was from the countryside and was in the agricultural department. Since he was poor, he was always busy teaching high schoolers to earn money. I listened to his difficulties, bought him dinner, and read the Bible with him. Since he liked chemistry, he transferred to another university a few years later. When he came back to SNU for his Ph.D. in chemistry, we met as a professor and a student. We had a long conversation about our life journey and future. Leaving behind the sad story of how he lost his first child, I wished that he could move on with his wife and a second child.

The other student attended a college of pharmacy. She cried a lot. She was lost and lonely. I prayed with her that God may strengthen her not to be lonely and weak. Several years later, I heard she got married after university, so I prayed that she could be happy in Christ Jesus with her family.

I remember my brothers and sisters in Christ still: Lee Ganghak, Choi Haemoon, Ahn Sun, Lee Junggook, Ryu Jeonghee, Kim Nankwon, Jo Yunhee, Seon Wonkyu, Kim Donggyu, and Ahn Eunyoung; they were my fellow peers; and Jeon Hotae, Jang Dalsig, Kim Mansoo, and Lee Ganglak were role models of our faith as older brothers. Now, they are professors or CEOs of enterprises. Ganghak went to the Graduate Theological Union seminary to study spiritual theology and is now a pastor and professor. Junggook and Jeonghee served as shepherds for several years and got married to study in Canada. Yunhee had a talent for helping people, so she went to Germany to study special education. She is now helping disabled and elderly people.

Now, we are all middle-aged and active workers in various fields of society and in church. We had the same dream. We vowed to do our best in our respective fields of knowledge with a burning passion until the gospel is fully proclaimed on Earth, until North and South Korea are reunited. Remembering them warms my heart.

On the way back home after a late Bible study, we came across my father selling some snacks on the street in front of the commercial bank in Shirm-dong. He handed out some rice cookies to each brother. We laughed, cried, prayed, and encouraged one another. I will never forget the beauty of that community serving God together.

Pain, pain, and pain

I accepted God with my head and heart, but there must have been something more required of me. I developed a pain in my lung during junior year. It took me an hour to walk from my house to the university. After I came back from school, carrying around a bag full of textbooks, I was exhausted and close to fainting. After a short break lying in bed, I went to tutoring. Maybe it was all too much work for me?

One day, while I was walking to class, I suffered a sharp stab of pain, and I could not breathe. Bearing the tremendous pain, I managed to walk to the campus clinic. A doctor called an ambulance to take me to the SNU hospital's emergency room. The doctor there told me that while walking on crutches, my lung and ribs rubbed together too long. The fatigue wore a hole in my lung and developed an air leak. I stayed in the hospital for two weeks after the pocket of air between my lung and ribs was removed. I went back home, but the pain started up again after a few days.

I was carried back to the emergency room again. Beside my bed, there lay a man in his late twenties. He was an athlete and had late-stage cancer. I gave him the Bible that I was reading and told him, "God will welcome you, brother."

I talked to him about Jesus Christ, the salvation and resurrection that I began to understand. He replied that he would read the Bible. We prayed together with sincerity.

The ER in the hospital was a real hell. A middle-aged man carried his wife on his back to the ER. She was rolling over on the ground from the pain, but the reception desk refused to accept her. It seemed as if some bureaucratic procedure were to blame. The man begged the doctors in the ER, then finally started to curse them. "We cannot be admitted to the hospital since we are poor, and you treat us like dogs? I wish North Korea would come down and kill everyone."

He left the hospital carrying his dying wife on his back. I asked a doctor why the hospital didn't accept her. He said, as if such happenings were commonplace, "The hospital will be in a permanent deficit if we accepted such people. It seems that she doesn't have much hope, anyway. Usually, such a man will run away without paying if she dies after the treatment."

I cried out in a rage. How could a doctor say such things? He said he could not do anything about it, either, and left. I didn't want to stay there anymore, and I got out of there. My family took me to Severance Hospital, where there was a renowned lung surgeon. They operated on my lung by opening up my ribs. I learned for the first time how immense pain can be when it comes every time one breathes. I was afraid to breathe. I could not breathe nor hold it. Either I have pain, or I die for want of air. I could feel the pain that Jesus had on the cross before his death. The pain reliever worked only a few hours, and it still hurt at night. It reminded me of Job. "Night pierces my bones; my gnawing pains never rest" (Job 30:17).

After several weeks, I got out of the hospital and went back home. Lying on my bed in my dark room, the only things I could do were praying and reading the Bible and books.

Perfect plan for an imperfect one

Lying in the basement room, I could hear footsteps on the road.

The light steps of elementary schoolers running and chatting with each other, the resounding clicks of women in high heels going to work, the rough steps of middle or high school students cursing each other, the lonely footsteps of drunken husbands late after work. Would they know that there is someone beneath the road, lying in the darkness? Even if I died that day, no one would know or care. If I were trapped there without knowing that there is a God, who is always smiling at me, I would have died out of despair.

Spring and summer passed away, and autumn came. I walked out of the dark room after several months. How transparent and blue was the autumn sky! How dazzling was the autumn sunshine, shining through the colored leaves! How crisply the autumn breeze scratched my cheeks! I realized how beautiful this world was for the first time. How thankful I was that I could breathe without pain and enjoy the warmth of the sunshine! The things that were so common that I hadn't even noticed! I learned in my heart that being grateful for everything is the will of God toward us in Christ Jesus.

Still, God wanted to purify me more. I felt the same pain in my other lung, which was X-rayed in the hospital. The doctor told me that it was the same symptoms as before and that I should have another operation. I was really disappointed. Again, I had to go through this pain for several months more? Why did God allow this to happen to me again?

"I need to ask God why."

The doctor looked at me incredulously.

"If you do not get the operation immediately, you could die of a heart attack when the lung bursts from the pressure!"

He emphasized *dying of a heart attack*.

"I am not afraid of dying. But I need to know the will of God for me."

I stepped out of the hospital. It was true. Regardless of death, I wanted to ask God how much longer and how much more I had to suffer. I stayed in bed for several days. I thought it would be better if I just went to God now.

"Shall I wait to die lying on a bed like this?"

I thought about ending my life without being noticed by other people. I couldn't do it. I could not make my mother cry, who loved me more than her own life. I decided to go to a prayer house.

I went to a prayer house on a remote mountain with my mother. There were many people, who had drowned in the sea of sickness and life's problems, gathered around to take a grip of the last help from God. Their pupils were empty of hope, despairing from the agony of life and flesh. I started to pray prostrated, settling at the corner of the praying hall. I didn't pray for a cure.

Instead, I started to grumble. "Why did you create me? Why are you so cruel to me? What worth am I to you if I lie down all day long, sick and useless? Now it is enough; please take me to you!"

One day passed. There was no sign of a cure and no answer to why I continued to live. I started to pray again. Suddenly, I heard someone singing a hymn behind me.

"And take me as I am, and take me as I am. My only plea, Christ died for me! Oh, take me as I am."

A sharp-edged sword pierced my heart! A cry burst out. My callous, unbending ego shattered into pieces. I cried and cried.

"Lord, forgive this wretch. A tiny, minuscule, stiff-necked creature argued with a creator because of a physical ailment. Please forgive my arrogance. An ignorant creature attacked you with little knowledge about my reason and purpose for being. Forgive my sin, Lord!" I repented.

"Surely I spoke of things I did not understand, things too wonderful for me to know...Therefore I despise myself and repent in dust and ashes" (Job 42:3,6).

I accepted God's lordship and sovereignty. My frailty, poverty, and suffering are all under the will of God. I realized that I have to comfort those who are fragile like me, give them hope, and not argue with God. This is the purpose of my life on Earth.

God saw through me. I felt uncomfortable when I read the verse:

"But who are you, a human being, to talk back to God? Shall what is formed say to the one who formed it, 'Why did you make me like this?' Does not the potter have the right to make out of the same lump of clay some pottery for special purposes and some for common use?" (Romans 9: 20, 21).

I wanted to say that God, who made me like this, is not just and that this is His responsibility. But I accept the verse as it is now. I am not a failure. Even though I am not perfect, the will of God in me is perfect.

"Lord, take me according to your will. I surrender myself to your hands to shape me."

The next day, I told my mother that we should go home. She had thought we would fast until I was cured, and she was surprised.

"Mom, I did not come here for a cure. I came here to know the purpose of my life. Now I know it."

I was certain that I could overcome any harshness in life through believing in God's love, no matter how difficult the situation might be. After coming back home, I prayed for five to six hours a day. I prayed the same prayer that Job did.

"But he knows the way that I take; when he has tested me, I will come forth as gold." (Job 23:10)

He cured me, indeed. My lung pain disappeared.

Many different faces of blessings

God taught me not to rely on the flesh. While I was ill and bedridden, I learned how to pray, how to read the Bible, and how to praise God in the midst of suffering. I came to know how Abraham, against all hope, believed in hope. Hope is not some rosy dream, but the belief that we never let go of in the depths of despair.

I could confess as Paul did in poverty and facing the threat of death: "I can do all this through him who gives me strength" (Philippians 4:13).

This confession became an existential declaration that keeps the faith in any circumstances, at the risk of my whole being. Coram Deo, the presence of God, made me realize how important it is to stand naked before God, with nothing to hide. How free life is once I fear no one except God. The life here is like a mist that will disappear soon; therefore, I do not obsess over things on Earth.

Rather, I live always fixing my eyes upwards. Now, I understand the verse, "Then you will know the truth, and the truth will set you free" (John 8:32).

I will not fear death if I look only at God. Free from the judgment of others and free from my desire for fame and money, everything is but an ephemeral flower except the truth of the cross.

"The longest hundred years!"

Life expectancies around the world are 100 years or less. I am already fifty-one, and how short the life is!

Often, we do not know why we are suffering. I learned from my struggles that instead of explaining where suffering comes from, God participates in our suffering. He was with me in the ambulance, with me in the ER, with me on the operation table. He stayed with me overnight when I was wailing in pain. I see the love of God when I see my mother suffering with me. Rather than rendering this world into a flawless paradise by His almighty rod, He humbled himself to be meek. His divine participation in human suffering is intemporal, since he embraced all of eternity in the presence of Jesus.

"Who, being in very nature God, did not consider equality with God something to be used to his own advantage; rather, he made himself nothing by taking the very nature of a servant, being made in human likeness. And being found in appearance as a man, he humbled himself by becoming obedient to death— even death on a cross!" (Philippians 2:6-8).

I carved these verses on my heart. I am still vulnerable to the weakness of the flesh, but God allowed me to learn to be strong by my weakness. Life is not about stepping back from the thirst of hope; rather, it is stepping forward in search of God's essence, rooted deeply in our soul. Also, life is laughing brightly through tears, however short, long, or lonely, relying on the love of brothers and sisters.

Most importantly, I learned how to hear His voice in the strong silence. God gave me the eyes of a Christian to see the blessings in bitter sufferings. Now, it is time to be mature in the journey of faith. As a mature child does not fight their parents, a mature Christian never argues with God. Like a grown-up child who can

With parents at Seoul National University graduation in 1990

read the mind of their parents, a grown-up Christian discerns the mind of God. A mature Christian never distrusts the love of God. They do not ask God to show His face. All He does for us is out of His love, even to death. I became mature through my illness. I sometimes stagger but never fall down. Afterward, my life became better, like the time I became a Homo erectus.

5

To Berkeley

In what torne ship soever I embarke,
That ship shall be my embleme of thy Arke;
What sea soever swallow mee, that flood
Shall be to mee an embleme of thy blood;
Though thou with clouds of anger do disguise
Thy face; yet through that maske I know those eyes,
Which, though they turne away sometimes,
They never will despise.
I sacrifice this land unto thee,
And all whom I lov'd there, and who lov'd mee;
When I have put our seas twixt them and mee,
Put thou thy sea betwixt my sinnes and thee.
As the trees sap doth seeke the root below
In winter, in my winter now I goe,
Where none but thee, th'Eternall root
Of true Love I may know.
(John Donne, *A Hymn to Christ*)

Like Daniel

After my illness, I returned to school for senior year. Since I was no longer strong enough to walk to school on crutches, I went to driving school. In driving school, they just taught the basic stuff. It did not help much. After I failed five times, I became the best driver and got my driver's license on the sixth try. Driving became natural to me. I bought an old secondhand Pony II with the money that I saved from tutoring. From time to time, the car stopped in the middle of a road, and people pushed the car from behind. But the car gave me much more freedom than before.

During my four years in university, I was in the first place in my department thanks to the wisdom that God provided me. In freshman year, I got Cs or Ds in physical education but did very well in other subjects. I concentrated on studying and faith and abstained from drinking, smoking, coffee, and dating. I think that was a good decision.

I formed a study group for my major subjects with three to four people to discuss lessons and do assignments together, building up logical thinking.

Mathematics is an abstract art of building one's logic based on the basic axioms, which makes it much different from physics, chemistry, or biology. It is a world of concepts where one can build up their own logical system, apart from experimental data and physical phenomena. Mathematics is the flower of reason given to human beings by God.

God gave me the creativity and quickness to approach mathematical problems differently. Sometimes, I got a perfect score when the average score among natural science students was around 20-30%. I willingly offered my answer sheets of problem sets to my peers, and they studied my manual to prepare for the exam.

Most of my university years were set in an epoch of fighting for democracy.[1] There was combat between demonstrators and the police every day. Tons of students died, and some of them burned themselves to death as a symbol of resisting tyranny. The song by demonstrators resonated across the Acropolis square in front of the library. I spent more time at Acropolis listening to speeches by students and social activists than studying in the library. Class boycotts and the conflict between students and professors made a regular university education and study difficult. The activists in my department asked me for help when they were organizing a protest. "Inkang, can you negotiate with the professors?" they would ask.

---

1 Between 1979 and 1987, university students and labor unions protested authoritative rule and martial law brought on after a military coup d'état led by Republic of Korea Army Major General Chun Doo-hwan.

I went to the professors' offices to ask for them to delay or cancel classes and exams, telling them that this was the era for the new world and asking them to understand our pure heart for democracy. Not all the professors agreed. Risking bad grades, we did not take our exams. Instead of studying, seeking the truth, and orienting our life, we spent our university life on resisting the tyranny and evil public forces trampling down the demonstrators. We suffered, stuck in the changing shift of society, politics, and history. But looking back now to that dark history, we were thirsty for the truth and courageously cast out our lives for justice.

Finally, we had a victory, and we were proud that we opened up a democratic government and expelled the military dictatorship. The world does not develop by itself. It needs sacrifice. I hope that such a history does not repeat itself. I pray that in the future, my children will not have to live with bloody political fighting and terrifying ideological combat; but that the time will come when one can dedicate their youth to art, faith, and pure study.

I was fascinated by topology and geometry. It requires brilliant ideas rather than computational machinery, and I decided to major in it. Mathematics suits me well. I don't have to deal with people, nor I need physical power. It is possible to do research while I am taking a walk, resting on the grass, or even while eating. I don't need to be in my office, nor the lab, nor the library. All I need is my brain, which frees up my time and space. Maybe I need a pen and a pencil occasionally. I finished my university life concentrating on studying and faith, as Daniel did over two thousand years ago. I encountered God, and I became His child. That was the most precious time in my life. I graduated university at first place in the department and second in the entire university, by the grace of God.

To Berkeley

I wanted to be a professor. In addition to teaching math, I wanted to give my students hope, teach them to dream, and help them learn about our Creator. Starting with the second semester of senior year, I started to prepare for TOEFL and GRE. I sent out applications to several universities in the States with a strong geometry and topology section. I needed a fellowship. Princeton and Harvard refused to offer me a fellowship, while the University of California, Berkeley, offered a scholarship and a living stipend. Some other universities offered a full fellowship for an entire year of my study. Since there were many prestigious professors in geometry and topology at Berkeley, I decided to go there. Berkeley has diversity in research and race, and furthermore, the weather was excellent. I wanted to avoid snow and rain since I used crutches. I was selected as a recipi-

With '79 Chevy in Berkeley in 1990

ent of an SK (Sunkyoung) abroad scholarship, and it greatly helped me. Jehovah-Jireh, as always He has been.

My mother worried. "Can you manage by yourself? I cannot go with you."

I was also worried. Someone had always helped me. But I did not want to be satisfied with the status quo. No challenge in life means no progress and no experience of God's guidance. And I knew it was time to learn how to be independent of my mother.

I flew in an airplane for the first time. I left Kimpo Airport with a bag full of books, clothing, and blankets, accompanied by a friend who would attend the same school. Yunhee, a sister in Christ with whom I studied the Bible at Kwanak ESF, had a brother living in Fremont, and he picked us up at the airport. We rode on a highway, with palm trees under the strong Californian sun and the smell of the Pacific Ocean, and arrived at his place in Fremont. He gave us a place to stay until we entered a dormitory at Berkeley. While we stayed there, we prepared for the preliminary exam, which would take place in two weeks. After I arrived in the States, I learned that since I was in the Ph.D. program, I needed to pass the preliminary exam within three semesters. I decided to take it immediately.

I needed a car. I passed the driving test and bought a '79 Chevy for $200. I glued a lever I brought from Korea to the pedal so that I could drive with my hands. One day, a friend and I decided to go to Berkeley for fun. I was driving the I-880 north when I heard a helicopter-like sound. I looked up at the sky, but there was nothing. The drivers passing by me were saying something and pointing their fingers at my car. I felt that something was wrong and pulled over. After I got out of a car, I realized what went wrong. The old rear tire had gone flat and was falling apart into pieces, causing the noise. I opened the trunk and found a spare tire. But I had no equipment to change it. I waved over a passing highway patrol unit, explained what happened, and asked for help. The officers said I had to tow the car. If insurance did not cover it, it would cost several hundred dollars. The car had cost only 200 dollars, and I could not afford to tow it. I asked them to change the tires since I had no equipment. They replied that the police did not do such things; however, they called Yunhee's brother to let him know what happened. After the police left, I waited for him for a long time, but he did not come. Walking along the road, I saw Mexican workers laboring on the freeway. I asked for help, and they changed the tire for me. We finally arrived at Berkeley safely. The city was quite impressive. Telegraph Avenue, where many vendors were selling weird stuff, was crowded with homeless people, street musicians, and hippies, and it smelled bad.

I was supposed to work as a TA and needed to take a practice teaching test lasting ten minutes. If I did not pass, I would have to take a language course. I went to the test, and three professors from the linguistics and education departments were there. They asked about some formulas and the process of proving them. I explained the solution, writing on a blackboard. They were impressed by how I could still write on the board while using crutches. They complimented my fairly good English, and my explanations were very clear.

"How long have you been speaking English?"

"Since middle school."

They shrugged.

"Pass."

I didn't take any private English lessons. All I did was take English courses at school, listen to AFKN, and read English novels, but I managed to communicate with people. After the semester began, I took the preliminary exam and the German language exam. The preliminary exam was as difficult as a math contest. Still, I passed both exams. That was a comfort from God to a timid child like me.

Even I dwell in the depths

I lived in a dormitory during my first year at Berkeley. The colt-like freshmen, who were free from their parents for the first time, gave me culture shock. The dorm was co-ed. There was only one shower room on each floor, and female students often came out of the shower half-naked. They were very sexually open. One day, I saw a nudist student come to a class naked and some people walking around naked.

"How could I survive here?"

I sighed. But I survived somehow. I got used to these things as time went by. My roommate, Trevor, was two meters tall and played the trumpet in the school band. He brought many friends into our room and played and laughed until very late, so I could not sleep very well. I encountered the same problems that foreign students usually have. Surviving in Berkeley was tough. There were many bright students, and it was intimidating to compete with them. I

At Sather gate of UC Berkeley in 1990

had to work on my assignments until late at night. Not just students, but professors also worked very late. Some of their wives divorced them, saying, "Don't come home, stay in your office forever!"

It was not easy to teach as a TA. My English was not fluent enough, and their slang was difficult to understand. Some students glared at me during the class, with their feet on the desks and with caps on. I warned them, "If you don't want to be in my section, please transfer to another section you like."

Some of them moved out of my section, and the atmosphere became much better.

Leading a class in English became easier after the first few weeks. Students also trusted me. They came to me during office hours, and we chatted not just about math, but also about their life. I counseled them. Some of them were very good in high school, but at Berkeley, they became nothing compared to other brilliant students. Even after getting admitted, about 30% drop out before junior year. Some of them got depressed and became addicted to drugs. Some students burst into tears in front of me, and I tried to soothe them as if I were their brother.

"Try your best first. After that, if you cannot follow the class, you can transfer to a university where you can do much better. You will have a better chance there."

Some of them followed my advice. Serving as a shepherd at ESF helped me a lot as a teacher. Precious life experience is like a secret key. It can open many doors one day.

It was not easy following graduate courses and serving as a TA at the same time.

Sometimes I struggled with some assignments for several days. I was exhausted from teaching, studying, and counseling young students. Every day after school around 5 pm, I went to the sea. I relaxed my tired body and weary soul by the wind of the Pacific Ocean. I walked along the sea at Berkeley Marina. I tried to hold myself up thinking about my mother and holding onto God. I recited Psalms sitting on the bench and looking at the sunset over the Golden Gate Bridge.

"Where can I go from your Spirit? Where can I flee from your presence? If I go up to the heavens, you are there; if I make my bed in the depths, you are there. If I rise on the wings of the dawn, if I settle on the far side of the sea, even there your hand will guide me, your right hand will hold me fast" (Psalm 139:7-10).

After I returned home, I prayed, read the Bible, and then wrote letters to brothers and sisters in Christ. I examined myself and pushed myself not to be weak and lazy. At the beginning of each class, I prayed for God's help, and He took care of me, indeed. On the teaching evaluations, the students gave me good scores. They liked that I prepared for class and explained things in an easy and clear way. They asked me to speak louder during class, though. I learned to rely on God in everything I did.

Ask questions if you want to succeed in your study

There are many brilliant people in the world. Sometimes, I did not understand the problems posed during seminars, but other students not only completely understood, but they asked questions and even suggested their own solutions. I thought about the problems at home after the seminars.

"Should I continue studying mathematics, or should I give up?"

As years passed by, and more brilliant students came along, I endured persistently. If I could not persevere, I couldn't finish my studies. If I focused on being brilliant, I would never be happy. In this world, there are so many brilliant people, like grains of sand on a beach. If I lingered on it, I would end up depressed or kill myself eventually.

For instance, on the ninth floor of Evans Hall, one can look out to the beautiful San Francisco Bay. Andreas Floer, who would have obtained the Fields Medal if he were alive, killed himself. I heard that he was constantly depressed since he thought he was not smart enough. It is well-known that he introduced the Floer homology.

Seoul National University had a passive teaching style, where professors wrote on the boards while the students copied down the proofs. At Berkeley, there were many discussions. They grasped the core of the argument during asking and answering.

If I did not understand something, I usually keep silent, but other students boldly asked questions. Of course, there were also many stupid questions.

"How come they do not know such easy things as a Berkeley student?"

But after a year, they knew more than I did. Korean students are quiet in class, even though they study a lot at home. Maybe it was because of their poor English, but Chinese students asked many questions even though their English was no better than ours. It made a huge difference eventually. A few minutes of conversation with famous mathematicians can help to get to the point of the problem. Even though I was shy, I started to ask more questions during the seminars. I give this piece of advice to future students:

"Ask anything. If you know the answer, respond bravely. It is better to have one conversation with an expert than to read a book a thousand times."

I heard of a Chinese saying: "It is better to be a fool for a few seconds by asking a stupid question than to be a fool forever not knowing the answer."

To geometric topologists, William Thurston and Mikhail Gromov were two icons. It is fairly well-known that their papers and books are dense and hard to read, but their surpassing insight and untraceable ingenuity are embedded in every line of their papers. Very often, a doctoral student works for several years on the details of a single line or paragraph of their papers to get their Ph.D. Thurston came to Berkeley as a director of MSRI from Princeton University. I attended his seminars often. I could understand the first five minutes, but everything after that was beyond my ability.

"Am I talented enough for math?"

I was worried but not despaired. Most students in the seminars felt the same way. I decided to read his Princeton lecture notes with two other students. It took me at least a full day or several days to figure out one line of his notes. Frankly speaking, I still do not understand some of the materials. I trained myself to convoke all possible mathematical imaginations to understand his lecture notes. Step by step, I gradually began to learn how to figure out

At Kingman Hall of Co-op house in 1992

my way out of the darkness. I passed a qualifying exam with some material from the notes and decided to do research on a problem related to hyperbolic geometry for my doctoral degree.

Wild party

No matter how difficult they are, most physical ailments and mental difficulties gradually disappear with time, leaving only a blurry trace. But the encounter with a person remains in the memory forever. I lived in a dorm my first year, but the next two years I stayed in a student-run co-op house. It cost less, but one had to work about five hours a week cleaning, cooking, and doing other house chores. Some co-op houses had really wild parties every weekend; a few houses were famous for doing drugs. I lived in a pretty, four-story house called Kingman Hall, clean of drugs. There were many young students, and I became their mentor.

I had bagels or cereal each breakfast. For lunch, either I returned to the house or had a simple meal near campus. We all had dinner together in Kingman Hall, prepared by the kitchen crew of the day. We were of different nationalities, different races, different cultures, and different family backgrounds. There was house manager Reba; a Mexican student who always wore a nice hat and could recite poems; kind King who had curly black hair; a girl with such big eyes who liked me a lot; a bit old British gentlemanly student who bowed to me always (I defeated him in chess once and after that he respected me); autistic John; a blonde girl who looked virtuous but had all kinds of sex toys in her room; a Japanese girl; my shy roommate; an Arab-American who had a Jewish girlfriend, causing constant fights with his parents; two students from the Middle east. One of them got a job at GM after graduating from Berkeley, and when he returned to the co-op for vacation, he said that America sucks the blood out of weak countries.

Mingling with them, I learned to embrace their culture and the way they think, without prejudice. I learned to view women as different people, not only as a different sex, by sharing the shower, restroom, and sometimes a room together. Such experiences helped me to make good friends with anyone, even with females, throughout my life.

American students looked immature, but they plan out their lives ahead of time. They estimated the cost and time to finish their degrees, and they carried out their plans accordingly. On the contrary, Korean students are too dependent on their parents. Even their majors are decided for them. Vaguely, they think that they have to enter good universities and then get jobs in big, major companies. However, their lives are theirs, not their parents'. Prestigious universities and famous jobs may not mean much in the long run. There is no heart or fun if it is not the road that they decided to take themselves.

My room was located on the lowest floor. Two beds and two desks took up most of the space, but I could look out the window to see the pretty trees. Just above my room, there was a dance and play room. A frantic party was held there every Friday. Noisy rock music and the smell of beer filled up the house. The party usually ended around 2 am, just after a police officer was called in by some neighbors to stop it. I usually went to a small cinema on University Avenue to avoid the hassle. Still, I do not like such noisy parties, filled with drinking and dancing. In Korea, university students also drank too much. I often saw many drunken university students vomiting and lying hungover on the road in Sinrim-dong area. Maybe they drank to forget the fear of the present and future, but it seemed like a waste of time and energy. Alcohol, dance parties, drugs, and sex do not fill up an empty heart. Maybe it seems to for a while, but after waking up, the emptiness only gets bigger and bigger. I totally agree with Saint Augustin that there is no genuine joy and peace to fill up the empty space of our soul until we encounter God.

With Casson and his students at his 60th birthday conference in 2003

6

Beauty of Mathematics

"Yes, but I'm not studying to become a tax collector, my father wants me to be a scribe," Gamesh pointed out. "Like him. So I don't see why I have to learn all this math."

"Because it's useful," Humbaba repeated.

"I don't think that's the real reason," Nabu said quietly. "I think it's all about truth and beauty, about getting an answer and knowing that it's right."

(Ian Stewart, *Why Beauty is Truth, A History of Symmetry*)

Casson

After two years of coursework, I chose Andrew Casson as my advisor. He does not have a doctoral degree; not from lack of ability, but because he was so smart while he was working on his doctoral degree at Cambridge, he became a professor before he finished his Ph.D. Later, he came to Berkeley as a full professor. He absolutely demanded that his students be independent researchers. After a qualifying exam, I went to his office.

"Why do you want a Ph.D.? Many people want to use their Ph.D. for something else after they get it. If you want to be my student, don't even think about it. A scholar is someone who lays down a foundation for himself. I warn you, I will not give any ideas about your thesis. I will not help you at all."

Some students actually left him since he did not help them, but I agreed with him about the attitude of a scholar. I remained as his student until I finished my degree.

Casson wrote about ten important papers. Some of them are written by his students, according to his lectures. He became famous after his work, the Casson invariant. But when I asked him about the invariant, he said he did not know. He told me to go to the library and read a book about the invariant written by one of his students. In conferences, if someone attributed some theorems to Casson, he didn't even know that he proved those theorems. He did not care about the credit.

For my thesis, he suggested a problem that he worked on for several years but had no clue about at all. It seemed dangerous to ask a beginning doctoral student to try it, but his intention was clear. A true mathematician should challenge any problem regardless of its degree of difficulty. Even if he fails, he will learn a lot of things from it. I walked through a long dark tunnel for two years to solve the problem. I could not even figure out where to properly start. Eventually, a professor at Stanford solved it, and I had to find another problem for my thesis.

In my third year, during a cozy, warm spring day, I was lying on the grass at Marina, and I was watching families and couples walking along the beach and hearing the children laughing and running. I was reading a math paper. I found a conjecture in the paper stating that the marked length spectrum of negatively curved Riemannian manifolds determines the metric up to isometry. I found out that the conjecture held true for dimension two. I wondered if the conjecture would be true for infinite volume hyperbolic 3-manifolds, since geodesics are filling up the manifolds in a complicated manner.

"Would it be true?"

Suddenly, I wanted to be the first to solve the conjecture for infinite volume hyperbolic 3-manifolds. I asked the students and Casson whether they knew the answer, but no one knew it. I learned that this conjecture was famous among the mathematicians who study negatively curved manifolds.

I decided to plunge into this problem for my thesis. I thought about the problem while I was walking, eating, and even listening to music.

"I solved it!"

I opened my eyes with such a joy, but I only saw a ceiling. It was a dream. I checked the logic while I was taking a shower, and found a serious flaw in the argument. I was disappointed. But after enough energy built up, I finally resolved the problem instantly. I found a formula relating the cross-ratio of four points in the ideal boundary of hyperbolic space to the lengths of closed geodesics. I obtained my doctoral degree under the title "Geometric structures on manifolds and the marked length spectrum," and received positive feedback from the math community. I was invited to a conference held in Switzerland and gave a lecture at a conference held in France. During the conference, I met French mathematicians Gerard Besson and Francoise Dal'Bo.

It takes me two to three years to resolve one math problem. A Thurston conjecture I solved recently took five years. In the 1970s, Thurston listed out several conjectures to be resolved. Accidentally, I found a clue to one of those conjectures, and I worked with two other mathematicians to solve it. After much trial and error, we finally found a solution generalizing his original conjecture. If we faced a wall, we stepped back and attacked the problem by a different route. Mathematicians need a lot of patience. It is a lonely job that no one can help with. Since we do not run experiments, our bodies may be free, but our heads are filled up with problems to be resolved while walking, driving, shopping, even using the bathroom. Once, while I was driving from Daejon to Seoul, I mentally solved a problem that took several pages of calculations. I was surprised that I could sort out such complicated logic while driving. Maybe a desire to be free of the problem and solve it pushed me to do so. My study at Berkeley was severe mental training. Casson used to point out errors when I was stuck with problems. Among jealous and competitive mathematicians, he was a real scholar.

Among other topologists at Berkeley, Robion Kirby is a four-dimensional topologist. He is famous for his Kirby calculus. I learned topology from him, and he helped me a lot during my Berkeley years. Even now, whenever I go to Berkeley, we have lunch together at La Val's, a classical place we often went to after seminars when I was a graduate student.

Peculiar Mathematicians

There are many weird mathematicians. One of them is Grigori Perelman, who solved the Poincaré conjecture 100 years after Poincaré raised the question.

When he was awarded the Fields Medal, he refused it and continued living in a shabby apartment in Saint Petersburg with his mother. If he had polished up his paper and published it in a journal, the Clay institute would have awarded him a million dollars, but he refused it also (The Clay Institute selected ten millennium problems such that anyone who could solve one of the problems would be awarded one million dollars). He put his preprints for the solution of the Poincaré conjecture on the arXiv and disappeared.

At Berkeley, there are also many peculiar mathematicians. William Thurston, who suggested a Geometrization conjecture (that every 3-manifold can be decomposed into irreducible factors that each piece admits one of eight geometries), attended Berkeley for his doctoral degree, and he became a full professor of Princeton at the age of twenty-eight. He came to Berkeley in my first year. It took me two years to understand his Princeton lecture notes. As an undergraduate, Thurston attended a small college in Florida. He earned an A in every course one semester and earned all Cs and Ds the other semester. When he applied to Berkeley, the selection committee was puzzled. Judging him by his transcript was difficult. One of his recommenders wrote:

"As far as I know him, he is not normal. I believe that he is a genius even though it is hard to tell whether he is good at math or not."

Thurston was admitted to Berkeley on those references. Not long after he arrived, he solved the most difficult problems on foliations. He can imagine the pictures that others cannot see. One of his students, who is now a professor at Chicago, told me a story. When he talked to Thurston about a problem that he had been wrestling with for two years, Thurston paused for a few minutes, looking far away, then suggested a solution immediately. In the presence of such genius, would there be anyone who was not intimidated, nor made to feel small? It seemed that he never prepared lectures. His explanations were reasonably easy for the first few minutes, only to suddenly switch to the pictures that no one but him could see. I could not understand it at all. He was awarded the Fields Medal in 1983, though most of his works are still in preprints.

I very often saw Mikhail Gromov at IHES near Paris. He is a living legend in modern geometry. His works on geometric group theory, symplectic and holomorphic geometry, and partial differential equation will forever remain in the history of mathematics. He looked like Tolstoy, with his bold hair and hairy mustache, and he was very kind to me. When I was visiting someone in Geneva with my family, we went to a restaurant downstairs and found him having a meal with his new girlfriend. He greeted me brightly and caressed my son Gunwoo's hair. But he is not always so kind to people. During a conference, a fairly renowned professor was giving a lecture. When he wrote down his theorem that he was going to talk about, Gromov interrupted and said that it would be trivial to show it. The professor was embarrassed, and his face blushed red. But he replied, gathering his courage, "Professor Gromov, it may look trivial to you, but it is not to most participants here. May I continue?"

Gromov left the lecture hall.

He stays in the States for several months each year. After his visit to Stony Brook University, he remarked, "A dog in Paris is smarter than the people there!"

It reminds me of Schopenhauer's saying: "With people of limited ability modesty is merely honesty. But with those who possess great talent it is hypocrisy."

Stephen Smale is one such genius. His work on a dynamical system is well-known, and he received the Fields Medal due to his work on the Poincaré conjecture for higher dimensions. Perelman solved the conjecture only for 3 manifolds, but Smale resolved it for dimensions at least 5. The Berkeley professor John Stallings also solved the same conjecture, but there is a rumor that Smale did it a few days before him. It is debatable. In the history of math, there are many such stories that an opponent solved a problem a few days, or even a few hours earlier.

Smale was a pacifist during the Vietnam War and kind of a hippie when he was young, and he solved the Poincaré conjecture on a Brazilian beach. It is said that he went to Brazil with an NSF grant to work on the problem. He played on the beach during the day, and he danced salsa during the night. Indeed, staying locked in an office does not help fuel the creativity required to solve a problem. Even when he was at Berkeley, he took trips to the Caribbean Sea on his own boat during summer. I heard that after he retired, he became a professor at the University of Hongkong and makes a lot of money.

Serge Lang, a Yale professor, used to visit Berkeley every summer. Once I heard someone fighting in the hallway of the math department. I went out of my office to see what was going on and found out that Lang was discussing math with another professor in a loud voice.

John Conway, a Princeton professor famous for knot theory and combinatorics, also has a loud voice. When he discusses math, he is so aggressive it looks like he's fighting. Every morning, he dropped by the same cafe to read the New York Times over coffee. I met him when I was staying at Princeton for my research one year. The door to his office was always open. It was written there, "Anyone is welcome."

I entered his office out of curiosity. It was filled with many paper mathematical models and a computer. The computer screen displayed a message that anyone could log in. But when I tried to log in, I found that the computer would only let me log in if I solved all the problems within a minute. The problems were like "what day of the week is January 2, 1948?". It was difficult to solve about ten problems within that time limit.

A professor in the Netherlands tended to forget everything else while thinking about a math problem. One day he was thinking about a problem while preparing his lecture, and he forgot to wear his pants and a shirt. He appeared in the lecture room in only his ties!

In Princeton University

It was my third year at Berkeley. Casson was supposed to lecture for a year at Princeton on 3-manifolds. Some of us followed him. I drove for a week with one of his students, crossing the country from west to east. We drove through Yosemite National Park, deserts in Nevada, the endless corn fields in the Midwest, and nameless small towns.

We arrived at Princeton late at night. We met Peter in the math building. He was calculating something about 4-manifolds in front of a computer, rocking his body back and forth. He greeted us curiously. He put us up for a night in his apartment, knowing that we had just arrived from Berkeley. His live-in girlfriend was a physicist.

When she heard that I am Korean, she said she knew a female

Korean student in her department. From hearing her story, I knew that the Korean student was in the first place nationwide in the entrance exam that I also had taken. After one year, she came to Princeton for her doctoral degree in physics, got depressed, showed

With friends in Princeton in 1994

severe unstableness, and finally, she disappeared. I imagine that the study did not go well as she planned, and she broke down.

When she entered Seoul National University in first place, all the mass media broadcasted exaggeratedly about her. Doing research and entrance exams are a different story. As she realized the gap between her real self and the expected image from the whole country, she lost confidence and finally collapsed. It was a sad story. Even unrecognized, if she could have built up her own academic world, it would have been much better for her. Unrealistic expectations crushed down her fragile soul. It showed how a competition-oriented society can destroy a good student. I hope wherever she might be now that she is happy.

Peter is now a professor at Princeton.

We could not find housing after that night, so we spent a week sleeping on desks in an empty classroom. Luckily, after a week, we found housing near the campus. The owner of the house was a medical doctor. The parents had bought a house for three daughters attending a nearby prestigious high school in the town of Princeton. I lived there for six months mentoring the girls, answering math questions, and listening to their life problems. I witnessed a wealthy American's lifestyle during my stay in the house.

One can feel free at Berkeley, but Princeton University has an elitist image. There was not even a movie theatre, and I had to drive 30 minutes to Trenton to see a movie. Berkeley accepts many students and expels about 30-40% of them afterward, whereas Princeton accepts only a few very good students from all over the world. I saw one student who could log into Conway's computer within 30 seconds!

There were many well-known professors at Princeton. Andrew Wiles, who solved the Fermat's last theorem, came to the department even on weekends. He missed the Fields medal, since he was forty-one when he solved the problem. John Nash, who is the main character in the movie "A Beautiful Mind," was walking around the library like a ghost. He has a mental problem, but he was awarded a Nobel Prize in economics, and Princeton University offered him a permanent office. Even though they were famous academically, most of them were aggressive. I gradually realized that to succeed in academia, one has to be fairly aggressive and active. But I did not like the attitude of being popular in the math community by solving problems competitively and by being attracted to only math problems. I believe that a true study is to discover the secret of God's creation and maintenance hidden in this universe and in a human being's reasoning.

Life together

I went to Inter-Varsity Fellowship after noticing a flyer on the wall for the Bible study. There were students from 7 different countries: America, Russia, Netherlands, China, Hungary, Wales, and Korea. We communicated in the American, Asian, and eastern European English accents. We understood each other since the central topic was God. When I prayed with a brother from Wales, I could hardly understand what he was praying about. I just answered "Amen" at the end of the prayer.

Henk, whom I met there, later worked in the lab in Cambridge in England. Now he is a professor at Bergen. He is 190 cm tall, and I looked tiny compared to him. He played piano very well. His father was a professor, and he told Henk not to be a mathematician since he did not have enough talent for math. So, he majored in physics at Princeton and did postdoc at Berkeley.

When I went to Cambridge for a conference, I stayed in his house, sharing our life and faith together. We went to a church that he was involved in and we prayed together about his relationship with his girlfriend. When I stayed in Paris, he visited us and played with Gunwoo very well. Gunwoo called him "ton ton Henk." When I met him in 2009 in Bonn, Germany, he already had gray hair. He shared a story to tell me how demonic the world could be to a person. He was harassed by colleagues for two years for the reason that he was not cooperating with them and that he did not comply blindly with the company policy. His hair turned gray due to the mental stress, and finally, he moved to the University of Bergen.

That winter at Princeton was the harshest winter in my life. I was imprisoned in the house due to the heaviest snow in 10 years. Pieter from the Netherlands, who was doing a postdoc at Princeton, came to my house to help me out. We went to the grocery store together and cooked together at my place, and we became good friends. Now he is at Max Planck Institute in Bonn. Whenever I go to Bonn, we see each other to catch up.

Following the IVF brothers, I went to an American church. I first tried an Episcopal church, which seemed like a Catholic church, but I did not feel comfortable with the service. Next, I tried an African American Presbyterian church. I liked their laughter, love and service atmosphere. But there were no young adults that I could mingle with. Finally, I went to a church just in front of the university.

The pastor of that church was a professor at Princeton Seminary. Most of the congregation were either lawyers or medical doctors. His sermon was very intellectually stimulating. The well-prepared sermon was elegant, well-organized and flawless with a clear logic, deep knowledge, and refined citations. But somehow, I did not experience the power of the gospel through the sermon. After the service, in fellowship time, people talked about a ski trip to Switzerland over a weekend and a journey to South America. Their life was far removed from mine. But it was good to experience a wealthy and cultured church once in my life. In the end, I settled in a church where most of the IVF members attended.

I met Eugene, a professor of history, in the Bible study group at the church. He graduated from Cambridge, but he had an Indian accent. We had discussions about the Christian life on campus, and how to live as a Christian professor and a Christian student. The biggest problem on campus was not persecution of Christianity but indifference about Christianism. Most people regarded Christianism as one of many values or as one of many religions. Because of this viewpoint, it was difficult to proclaim that a Christian life is valuable to society. Homosexuality was emerging as a big issue in the church. The church did not have a strong stance on homosexuality, abortion, and divorce, but it passively responded and was observed in secular cultures. We fervently discussed how to overcome this difficult situation and how to live out our faith actively in current society. There were no definite conclusions, but we agreed that the Christian is not just a nominal noun; rather, it should be a verb defined as living according to the commands of God.

Casson did not like Princeton very much. We came back to Berkeley after a year. On the way back, I drove together with a Princeton seminary student that I met in the church. We drove the southern part of the country near route 40. Those parts did not look like the America that I had known so far. We passed through poor areas in Mississippi. Southern Afro-Americans called us 'sir' during conversations. A white man that we met in a poor village sighed, telling us that there are only gambling, drinking, and women in that village. Those villages clearly showed the problems of race, poverty, and decadence existing in America. There are many things that I learned by crossing the country twice. I envied the immense and rich land with beautiful nature, which are all the gifts of God. I also saw the poverty of culture, with McDonald's and motels everywhere, contrary to the European scenery.

I have precious memories of my time at Princeton: such a beautiful campus, covered with colored leaves in autumn, the serene river covered with white snow in winter, with tall trees that were seen from my room, the snow flowers on trees, a small creek that I used to visit alone in spring and summer; the house of Einstein and small cinemas in Trenton; Linda, who read Thurston's lecture notes together with me in a tea room several times a week. A year at Princeton, sometimes struggling with math, sometimes jumping with joy when I figured out the solution!

Brothers in Christ were a good source of strength wherever I was. We tasted the beauty of life by eating together, comforting together, and encouraging together.

With these beautiful memories, I also have a painful memory. Before I moved into a dormitory, I rented a room for a month in a couple's apartment from China. The husband was doing post-doc. I set up an answering machine in my room, and one day it recorded a conversation of his wife by accident. If I do not pick up the phone in 10 seconds, the machine started to record the message or conversation. After they learned that the conversation was recorded, they broke into my room and smashed the machine on the ground. I explained how the machine works several times, but they did not listen. I was so upset but felt sorry for them about how closed and suspicious their minds were after the cultural revolution of the 1960s. If they cannot trust anyone, it is like living in a cemetery. They are afraid of something unexpected coming out of the darkness. If I, like a ghost, cannot talk to anyone, cannot pass love around, cannot trust anyone, then it is not a community. The kingdom of God is in the community of faith. It reminded me of some phrases from the book "Life Together" by Dietrich Bonhoeffer.

> *"'Behold, how good and how pleasant it is for brethren to dwell together in unity'-this is the Scripture's praise of life together under the Word. But now we can rightly interpret the words 'in unity' and say, 'for brethren to dwell together through Christ.' For Jesus Christ alone is our unity. 'He is our*

peace.' Through him alone do we have access to one another, joy in one another, and fellowship with one another."[2]

Looking back a year at Princeton, I remember Henk, Brian, Paul, and Mattias, in Christ Jesus. The community of love in Christ is a model of heaven in this world.

Whenever I go on a trip where they live, I still contact them to pray together.

The Beauty of Mathematics

I think that mathematicians are like artists and philosophers. They need creativity and perseverance, and they have to express their work in a way that is accessible to people. Another common factor is that no matter how hard they explain it, people do not understand them! It's a joke. I think that the beauty of mathematics is freedom. Maybe many people would not agree with it. They will say that even thinking about math gives them a headache. They probably never enjoyed mathematics. In Korea, there is one supplementary math book known to high school students. Rather than studying it, many students use it as a pillow. After the entrance exam, the book is thrown out for recycling. Only the first few pages are darkened, but the rest are never looked at. It is even depicted in some cartoons, where a person with a sleeping problem immediately falls asleep when he sees the book. That is the tragic reality in Korea for students who study math only for the exam.

If you study mathematics seriously, you will realize that math is the subject of absolute physical and mental freedom. You don't need another's help, nor a laboratory, nor a computer, which is essential in a modern society. There is no restriction on space. One can do math while walking, eating, or even while driving. If you drive a car with a mathematician, something funny will happen. If he is a number theorist, he will analyze the license plate number in front of you.

---

2 Bonhoeffer, Dietrich. 1993. Life Together. New York, NY : Harper & Row Publishers, 1993.

"Hmm...if one multiplies the numbers, it will be a square of a prime number, and if one adds them up, it is a square of a perfect number!"

There is a well-known topologist, R. Bing, who was a president of AMS. He was also a deacon in a church. There was a famous story about a stormy night when he was driving a car with several mathematicians. He was explaining a theorem to them while driving. They could barely see outside, since the car windows were all fogged up. It was sleeting heavily, and the road was icy. He should have driven carefully, as all the passengers were scared to death. Finally, Bing leaned forward as if he wanted to clean up the fog from the windshield. But he continued his explanation, driving the car with one hand and drawing pictures, arrows, and symbols on the windshield with the other. The lifespan of all the passengers must have shortened ten years from fear of death!

One needs imagination to resolve a difficult math problem. The clue is a brilliant idea. The first step is to sort out a method and machinery to attack the problem.

This process is very important. To make the first step, we let our imaginations run. Try this and that way, and if something is tangible, then we develop the theory rigorously. Sometimes we reach a dead end after a few months or a few years, even if it looked promising. Then, we search for another way. We repeat this process several times until we find a solution.

We call a person who quickly solves a problem a genius. But mathematics does not necessarily need just geniuses, but it also needs average people. An average person like me sometimes solves a problem that a genius cannot solve. A genius sometimes runs so quickly that he misses many details. An average mathematician fills this gap. In that process, an unexpected result may come out.

The most required virtue in math is freedom from given frames. Since someone tried out non-Euclidean geometry, denying axioms for Euclidean geometry, a hyperbolic geometry came out. From this nonstandard geometry, a theory of relativity for viewing this universe in 4-dimensional Minkowski space was possible.

If we had insisted only on Euclidean geometry, we would still exist in an age of horse-drawn chariots and of fear of falling off the edge of the Earth if we traveled too far.

It is the same for philosophy. The empiricist did not believe that the thing does exist outside of me, but the rationalist like Descartes, who believed in reason and knowledge, believed that one can understand the essence of things by reasoning and inferring. But Kant eventually argued in "The Critique of Pure Reason" that "What can we know?"

The answer, if it can be stated simply, is that our knowledge is constrained to mathematics and the science of the natural, empirical world. Extending knowledge to the supersensible realm of speculative metaphysics is impossible.

The method to approach a problem in mathematics also depends on viewpoint.

In mathematics, when introducing a new concept, it is helpful to combine these two philosophical methods, Hegel's method. The Copernican revolution advances mathematics, not just philosophy. Art is an emotional expression of a flower of free imagination, but mathematics is a logical expression of a fruit of free imagination. The reason I say *fruit* is that we can touch it and feel it and taste it in reality. Many people think that mathematics is just a bundle of pure logic and concepts. They think that mathematics is useless after graduation from a university, but there are many advantages of mathematics in our daily life.

Many parents force their children, who want to study math in depth, to be medical doctors or lawyers or something else for practical reasons. It is not bad to be a mathematician. Furthermore, symbols and numbers are common languages in the world. If you can speak a little bit of their language, you can get a job anywhere in the world as a mathematician.

Some people ask me what Topology is. It is a branch of mathematics which studies the essential shape of things. For example, a donut has a hole, but a ball does not have any. They are different topologically. It does not matter how round or how smooth they are. It does not matter whether they are made of rubber or flour. Only the number of holes matters. If one deforms a shape of a doll made out of clay, as long as one does not tear it apart or glue it together, the deformed one is topologically the same. Deforming does not destroy the essential shape (*Ding an sich* in German).

In more practical terms, to a topologist, whether someone has a long nose or a flat nose, is not important. If that person has a nose, it is enough. A Western nose and an Asian nose are all topologically the same (homeomorphic in mathematical terms). To God, whether a person is Western or Asian, white or black, poor or rich, tall or short, disabled or not, old or young, educated or not, it is not important. He or she is a lovely child of God.

Then what's the use of Topology? It has many uses. Most com-

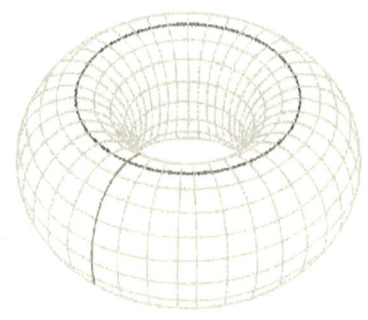

monly, by capturing the essential shape of a person wanted for a crime, one can use Topology to search for that criminal. It can also be used for recognition of fingerprints, topology of networks, design of semiconductor circuits, etc.

On the other hand, distance and smoothness are important to geometers. Topology does not care whether the linen is wrinkled or ironed, but geometers are sensitive to this. There could be infinitely many different smooth structures with the same topology. The real line and the open interval between 0 and 1 with usual topology are the same to a topologist, but metric-wise, they are much different to geometers. Topologists are generous to people about how they dress and how they appear, but geometers are picky about the appearance, outfit and height of people. But sometimes the sharp critical eyes of geometers could be much more effective than those of topologists. One example is the solution of the Poincaré conjecture that was recently resolved. Topologists could not resolve the problem for a hundred years, but a geometer, Grigori Perelman, used the geometric evolution of Ricci flow to resolve the problem.

Studying math makes a person more logical. If a person is logical, he will logically estimate the consequence of his acts and thoughts. If people can behave logically, society will be more orderly and safer to live in with fewer crimes. Illogical thinking brings chaos, crime, and violence. The morals and rules that we have to observe are based on logical regulations.

These are the more visible fruits of mathematics. Without mathematics, there are no bridges, no cars, no airplanes, no buildings.

Sometimes mathematics leads people to God through logic. As a mathematician, I feel the limitedness of our logic. Empirically, I realized that I cannot reach the truth by myself. I am speaking for myself. That is one of the reasons that I bow down before the absolute God, who surpasses our logic and reason.

If one studies the dimensions, it is very inspiring. One can see things in dimension 3 even though they are not visible in dimension 2. More accurately, more tricks are possible in dimension 3. A knot in dimension 3 is an unknot in dimension 4. Christopher Zeeman proved that a knot in a lower dimension is an unknot in higher dimension. Isn't it inspiring?

All the problems that we have on earth can be resolved by God, who lives in a higher dimension. That is why we have to pray to God in heaven when everything around us is blocked. Some might ask how it is possible that an infinite God can come to earth as a human being. It is possible since he lives in a higher dimension.

It is logically possible for a Christian mathematician.

Secret of God hidden in mathematics

You likely learned about zero and infinity in middle school and beyond. Indeed, if you think about infinity, it does not exist in this world. The number of atoms in the universe is finite. Nothing can be infinite. The number of things existing in the universe is between zero and infinity. I can make something finite from finite things. But we cannot make one out of zero. The number zero and infinity belong to God. Hence the being that can make a finite thing out of zero must be a being that contains infinity, the creator. Since the creator created everything out of nothing, the creator must contain infinity. Hence God lives in an infinite dimensional space. Let us think about zero and infinity, keeping this in mind.

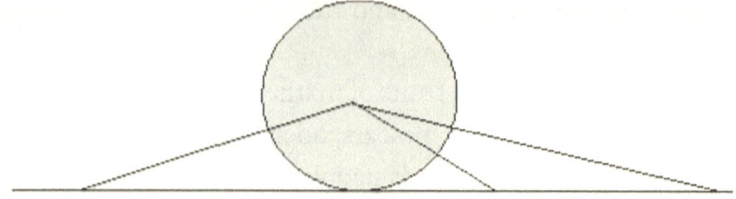

Draw an open interval (0,1) on a piece of paper. There is a one-to-one correspondence to the whole real line from (0,1). To see this, cut out a cord of one inch and bend it into a half circle. Put this on the paper, and draw a line passing through the bottom of the half circle. Draw rays from the center of the half circle to the line to see that there is a one-to-one correspondence from a half circle to the line. What I am trying to say is that (0,1), and the real line is homeomorphic in mathematical terminology. Suppose this universe is 4 dimensional, including time (most people agree that this universe exists in a finite dimensional space). Imagine that (0,1) represents the coordinate axis for time, which is equal to the whole real line as we have seen already. Draw (0,1) on a sheet of paper. A person, who exists in 3-dimensional space, can look at this from the beginning to the end of time at the same time. God is like this. Since God exists in infinite dimensional space, or at least in more than 4-dimensional space, he can see the history of human-beings from the creation to the final advent of Jesus simultaneously. If the whole universe, including time, is contained in a sheet of paper, as we can reach any spot of the universe with a pencil, God can enter into any space at any time of history of human beings. It is by the same principle that Jesus entered the upper room after his resurrection. It is possible, since God exists beyond the dimension of the universe and time.

In Genesis 1:1, "In the beginning God created the heavens and the earth."

Some people ask, "What does beginning mean? If it is the beginning of time, then what is before that?"

If God put time between 0 and 1 in a bigger space, to God it is just one second. Since we live inside time, to us, it is always infinite. But to God, time exists as a finite part of a bigger dimensional space. We may understand the following verse in this context: "But do not forget this one thing, dear friends: With the Lord, a day is like a thousand years, and a thousand years are like a day" (2 Peter 3:8).

God can choose time as (0,1) or (0,2) as he wants. That is why there is no restriction of the length of time with God. We have to keep this in mind when we read Genesis. A day to God could be a thousand years or a hundred thousand years to us. Plato said, "We only look at the reflection of a thing whose ideal being exists only in heaven." God is outside the finite dimensional space and time, but we are trapped inside.

It is not easy to know him perfectly. We cannot escape this space and time. That is why God, through the incarnation, came to the space and time where we live. Since we did not understand him correctly, he showed himself to this world in the form of flesh. To understand his humbleness, let us look at the following example. We live in a 3-dimensional space. We cannot live in 2-dimensional space, even if we were to try. No matter how hard we try to be prostrate, we cannot be completely flat. How much suffering and inconvenience must God have had to go through, who exists in an infinite dimensional space, to come to 4-dimensional space?

But why did God make Adam and Eve 3 dimensional figures, and not 1 or 2-dimensional figures? There is a partial differential equation called the "Maxwell equation," which makes modern physics possible. Usually, the movement of the light is explained using this equation. For this equation to work well, one needs at least 3 dimensions. That is why God created a 3-dimensional physical space where light and the electromagnetic field can work properly, and a 1-dimensional time-space so that one cannot jump around in time, resulting in a 4-dimensional space and time. If God had this equation in mind, he created Adam as a 3-dimensional figure so that he can live in a world where the beautiful light is shining. But why not 6 dimensions or 8 dimensions?

As I already mentioned, there is a 3-dimensional Poincaré conjecture whose solution was given by G. Perelman recently. This Poincaré conjecture for higher dimensions had already been settled. Only 3-dimension was unsettled for 100 years. In geometry and topology, 3 and 4 dimensions are most difficult dimensions to deal with. If the dimension is high, there is much space to move around, and topology gets easier, but geometry gets difficult. If the dimension is low, geometry gets easier, but topology becomes difficult. It is in 3 and 4 dimensions where both geometry and topology get difficult. That is why God puts the universe in 3 dimensions and time in 1 dimension so that the operation of the universe and time is mysterious and human-beings live in an astonishing 3-dimensional world!

In ancient times, most mathematicians were philosophers. Mathematics was developed very early in India, China, and Babylonia. Well-known Greek mathematicians studied geometry in Egypt, algebra in Babylonia. Thales, Pythagoras, and Plato studied in Egypt. The work of Archimedes, which exists until now in a published form, are math papers which describe the discovery of π, the area of a circle, the area of a sphere, the volume of a sphere, etc. In the paper "Measurement of a Circle," he calculated the value of π. In "The Quadrature of the Parabola," Archimedes proved that the area enclosed by a parabola and a straight line is 4/3 times the area of a corresponding inscribed triangle. He expressed the solution to the problem as an infinite geometric series with the common ratio 1/4.

His method became a root of calculus, discovered by Isaac Newton two thousand years later. In ancient Greece, Euclid's "Elements of Geometry," Apollonius' "Conics," and Diophantus' "Arithmetica" are landmark achievements. Aristotle and Plato both studied mathematics and philosophy. Plato allegedly put a note in front of Plato's Academy lecture hall, "Let no one ignorant of geometry enter here."

Mathematics describes the law of God's operation of the universe. Kepler thanked God after the discovery of what is known as Kepler's law: "Creator and Lord, I give thanks to you for making me happy by the greatness of your work!"

Leibniz said, "The universe is created by the calculation of God." and Plato prayed to God, who always behaves geometrically.

But mathematics is not perfect. Kurt Gödel proved the imperfectness of mathematical systems, known as "incompleteness theorem." It means that there exists a rational world beyond the proof of mathematics, and that world cannot be proven, but is a realm of faith and choice. This proclaims to all the modern scientists using mathematics that we must be humble before God.

Indeed, Gödel tried to prove the existence of God. Gödel confessed that he was a Lutheran. He put God as a being having all positive characteristics. In the Bible, God is described as being generous and the source of goodness.

I also do research on mathematics, which is a part of the wisdom of God who created the universe, sustains it, and reigns over all things in it with immeasurable wisdom. The more I study mathematics, the more overwhelmed I am by the grandeur of his wisdom, and I bow down before him since the infinite God talks to me, a finite being, with infinite goodness.

I experience the greatness of God through mathematics. I touch a small bit of his wisdom through it. When I solve a problem which may have lasted several years, I thank Him that he showed me his wisdom with his mercy. I discover the beauty of the world through mathematics. A day passes quickly when I think about math. It is the time when I talk to the secrets of God hidden in this universe. Today, I talk to God to find his wisdom and the beauty hidden in the world.

"Dear Lord, who is the source of wisdom and knowledge,

please reveal the secret of the universe in your mercy so that I can share the beauty of the universe that you created with all the people on earth."

7

Beautiful Hidden Flowers

Not every flower blooms like a flower.
If it blooms in a hidden place, it will be brighter.
(Cheon Yanghee, *Hidden Flower*)

Amber

I started to do one-to-one Bible studies with friends at Berkeley. I taught anyone who wanted to read the Bible, regardless of their nationality, American, Indian, Korean, Dutch. I had an Indian friend, Amber. He had a Hindu background, but he was not a devoted Hindu. He liked to bird watch with his deep, dark eyes. I went to his place early on Sunday mornings. He had asthma since he was young and had difficulty waking up early in the morning. I would read the Bible while he was getting ready, and sometimes we would have pancakes together for breakfast. Surely, there were cultural gaps between us, but we tried to find a universal image of human beings in the Bible, and we talked about God and the salvation of humanity. I prayed for him after the Bible study. I hoped that the seed of faith planted in his soul would grow and bloom someday.

After a qualifying exam, I visited him for a week. Both his parents were professors and members of high society. They employed more than ten maids and servants. They prepared breakfast in the morning, cleaned house, and brought out tea and goat milk after the siesta in the hot, greater than 40 degree Celsius afternoon. I felt that I was being treated like a king because I only ate spaghetti, salad and orange juice during my Berkeley years. I did not feel totally comfortable with getting such service even though they are not slaves, but they are paid for their work, and that is one of the ways of creating jobs in India. Amber's brother had a hearing problem, and he listened to me by reading my lips. Maybe that is why Amber treated me very naturally even though I had a disability. Now, he is married with one child. I was happy to hear that he became a professor near New Dehli. I thank God for all this, and I would like to visit him again if I get the chance.

Sam

One day, after a dinner in a unit 2 dormitory, there was a student who came to my room. He saw me in the cafeteria at the beginning of the semester, and he felt like talking to me. We talked until late at night, and then he returned to his room. He was majoring in philosophy. Sam and I had many common interests and similar thoughts. We became friends. We talked about everything—our life, hope, and this world while we took walks along the Marina. We went to movies, concerts, and exhibitions together. His heart was pure like an idealist, and he had deep thoughts. He even wanted to make a movie.

"If I can ever make a movie, the first movie will be about you, Inkang." Since he liked movies, we saw *The Unbearable Lightness of Being, Dances with Wolves, Dreams, Seven Samurai, Wild Strawberries, Persona*. We shared opinions about movies which are sometimes surrealistic, vague or even immoral. I visited his house in L.A. a few times. He had a dark pain. His father was a poor pastor, and his mother suffered from schizophrenia for a long time. Nonetheless, we encouraged each other that we must be genuine pioneers of the world.

One day Sam brought a silver flute to me. He had listened to someone playing flute in a BART station, and the sound had enchanted him. He went to a shop and bought a flute for me right away.

"It will be wonderful if you play a flute."

Whenever I play the flute that he gave me, my heart becomes warm over the thought of Sam. After several years at Berkeley with me, he left for Boston to work on a master's degree in seminary.

When I came back to Berkeley in the summer of 2005, I called Sam. I drove down to Monterey from Berkeley and Sam drove from L.A. He cried and hugged me tightly. My heart melted to see that he had aged so much. We talked for several hours sitting on the white sand of Monterey beach. He was working as a teacher in an elementary school for troubled children. He helped children with his own money because the support from the government was not enough. He became outraged at how harsh this world is to the poor. He talked about his girlfriend, who had cancer, worried about his parents getting old, and wanted to study film but could not afford it. He was tortured between the reality of things and his dreams. I did not know how I could help him. I prayed for him that God, by His almighty hands, would guide him through his life for the best.

With church members in Berkeley in 1991

Colleen

I was tired of hearing rock music every Friday night at Kingman Hall. I preferred classical music. I frequently went to a concert hall on campus, and I listened to classical music while I was studying. I like the second movement of Beethoven's *The Emperor*

Concerto that I used to listen to at the Marina when I was mentally exhausted. I had a dream that someday I will play that serene melody, after the stormy waves of life. I put up a note on the bulletin board in the music department. "If you give me a piano lesson, I will teach you mathematics."

The next day, someone called. It was Colleen. She said that, somehow, she was drawn to the note and it made her call. She had light brown hair with a bright face. She was eighteen years old from Wisconsin. I rented a piano. Colleen came to my house twice a week and taught me the basics. It was the first time in my life I had tried to play the piano. I advanced quickly since I already knew guitar chords.

In fact, Colleen entered the math department at first. She even competed in WMO (World Math Olympiad) at the high school. But one day, during a math class, she wondered how it was possible to help people with mathematics. Hence, she transferred to the music department to serve people with music. She had played the piano since her youth. She was interested in music therapy. During the weekdays, she served lunch to the homeless, and on the weekends, she went to nursing homes to play piano for the elderly. She gave a free lesson to anyone who wanted to learn piano.

Colleen taught me for six months. When she had an audition, I drove her to it and watched her play. I encouraged her instead of her parents. I learned to play the first movement of *The Moonlight Sonata*. I can still remember us going together to the trumpet concert by Wynton Marsalis and the Coriolan Overture by Beethoven.

The decline of morality in America is disappointing. But the power of supporting America comes from good people like Colleen and Sam, who serve people without any reward. It is the same in Korea.

There are many beautiful hidden flowers who live without name and glory, but just fix their eyes on Him according to the will of God.

My Savior, My Lord!

I met many wonderful brothers in Christ at the Korean church that I attended at Berkeley. Sooyun, Alex, Inho, Sugchul, Soonhoi. I miss them a lot. Sooyun drove me to the church the first time in his big old car. He was waiting for me in front of dormitory unit 2. He also took me to his old apartment to have dinner together. Even though all we had was rice and kimchi, we encouraged each other during our Berkeley years. After graduation, he got a job at Livermore lab but is now living in Oregon. Whenever we meet in Korea or in the States, we pray for each other.

Sugchul was my fellow cell member at Berkeland church. He often brought a lunch bag for me, and we had lunch together on the grass in front of Evans Hall. He was weak in faith, and I prayed for him a lot.

Soonhoi was a cell leader. We worked in the same school at SNU (Seoul National University) for a while, and he is also a part-time minister. He also leads the worship on campus each Wednesday, and I gave sermons there a few times at his request.

Alex, with his hair in gel, was an emotional guy. We were lonely singles and often met in a café to chat. Now he is a busy father, a leader in Berkeley Lab, and a leader in his church. I once visited there. The congregation was full of passion for missions abroad.

We lived as brothers and sisters in Christ. Our faith was pure and sincere. With good hearts, we helped the newcomers. To proclaim the gospel to a brother and to help him to accept Jesus, we shared our lives and prayed together until dawn. We did it out of pure hearts for the sake of others.

But sometimes the church would be impatient with people because of its zeal for proclaiming the gospel. The church would reorganize the system and programs to make their plans work. They made a list of commandments to follow. Even though Jesus took three years to train twelve apostles, they planned to evangelize several hundred at one time. Such a mass endeavor could destroy a pure love for them. One has to wait for someone to be born again in their inner being after conversion, but we try to push those who are weak in faith to live up to a standard of rules.

When we face God, he will ask us about the depth and weight of our love. He will ask us whether we carried out our preaching, serving and dedication out of Jesus' love, being faithful only to God, not out of our zeal and desire to accomplish our own plans. Jesus died on the cross out of love for us. Even if we have the tongue and wisdom of an angel, even if we lay down our lives for the gospel, it is a difference as big as heaven and earth whether we did it out of love, or out of our zeal.

God's community cannot be built just by having good programs. Sinners like us, who are impossible to love, do our best by the power of the Holy Spirit, with love and patience, to build the community of God, and that is the real community of God. If the weak and the poor leave the church, something is wrong with that church. Jesus was with sinners, the weak and the poor. However, the church on Earth cannot be perfect. We should love the imperfect church as a body of Christ.

I was baptized in this church. I confessed my faith in front of the congregation.

"You are my Savior, you are my Lord, and you are my Friend and Lover!" I wept in my heart once again.

Mother Teresa

Too much classwork, research, and church activities burned me out, and I developed a pain again in my lung. If I work one day, I needed to rest two days. Sometimes I lay sick in bed for several days. It was around Easter when I took my qualifying exam. The pain in my lung became excruciating two weeks before the exam. I went to a clinic on campus, and the doctor told me that I should stay in the hospital. But I relied on God again. I prayed until Easter was over.

"Please God, I pray to you to take care of me with my weakness..."

I dared to rely on God instead of a doctor, and each time God cured me and revitalized me. I passed the qualifying exam also. Weak health was like a thorn in my body. This thorn served to make me an instrument of God and to purify my soul and to make me depend humbly only on God.

I went to India during the summer vacation after the qualifying exam. Because I bought the cheapest ticket I could find, there were five stopovers on the way to New Dehli. At the New Dehli airport, something unexpected was waiting for me. At customs, they refused to allow me to enter India since they found a problem with the visa. Some of the numbers on the visa were smeared, and they couldn't read it. They took me to a room. I said several times that I got the visa from the San Francisco Indian embassy, but they did not listen to me. They asked the same question over and over again for an hour. Later I learned that that was a common occurrence

In India in 1993

when asking for a bribe. Since I did not know that, I resisted until the end, and finally, they let me enter the country.

For a month, I traveled to New Dehli, the Taj Mahal in Agra, the Rajasthan area, and to Calcutta. In Rajasthan, I visited a Jain center and had a conversation with a monk for an hour. They wore a mask so as not to kill any bacteria in the air and swept the floor in front of them when they walked to avoid stepping on small creatures. Their way of seeking the truth was abstinence and asceticism. Those in the Jain center were struggling against the desires of their flesh to seek the truth. It seemed extremely difficult to live like that. Can we be free from our sinful nature by asceticism? I wished to proclaim the following gospel to them also:

> *"Come to me, all you who are weary and burdened, and I will give you rest. Take my yoke upon you and learn from me, for I am gentle and humble in heart, and you will find rest for your souls. For my yoke is easy and my burden is light." (Matthew 11:28-30).*

Everywhere in India, children followed me saying "Kaku, Kaku" and asking for money. Many people were living on the street with only one scoop of dirty water and a piece of roti (flat bread) for a day. I had never seen so many people in that state before. Even as a student, I was much better off compared to them. All unhappy people should travel to India. The poverty, caste system, divided religions and different language are all stumbling blocks for India. Even the rich and long history of India is held back by those things. India was stuck in the low gear of a tough history.

I crossed the Rajasthan area on a camel. On sunny days, the

With Indian friends in Calcutta in 1993

temperature reached around 50-60 Celsius. We met a sandstorm on the road. I could not breathe. I lay down on the ground behind the camel with my face covered with a towel. After an hour, the storm was gone, but the landscape was completely changed. I watched the sand dunes under the moonlight, and I was half-dreaming when I heard the loud prayers coming from the Hindu temples. I traveled for a month fighting against the heat and my physical weakness. But I felt sorry for the Indian people, who got so used to the poverty and their fate, and I was sorry that I could not do anything for them. I thought, what's the use of mathematics and doctoral degrees to these people? I faced the same problem that Colleen did. I was getting exhausted.

I took a train to Calcutta to visit the centers for the poor and the sick run by Mother Teresa. Those centers for abandoned children, and for people facing death, were run by volunteers and nuns. I was waiting for Mother Teresa at the doorway. A small nun with a bent back came up to me when she found me.

"Why did you come here, my son?"

"I am tired of my life." And I added, "Do you think you can change the world by taking care of the sick in this corner of Calcutta?"

Indeed, that was a question for myself. I felt indebted as a person who knows the grace of God. I have to do something historically great for God. But I felt so small in front of this absurdity in India. How much help would it bring to this world to take care of a small number of people here while there are so many people on the street living and dying in poverty and illness?

She replied peacefully, "My son, it is not my duty to change the world. I am just faithful in small things." She invited me to a chapel and prayed for me not to be weary about life, but to be faithful in small things.

She taught me to do small things that I can do now even if I have a great vision to change the world. She gave me a small card, where it is written:

The fruit of Silence is Prayer.
The fruit of Prayer is Faith.
The fruit of Faith is Love.
The fruit of Love is Service.
The fruit of Service is Peace.

With my mother in 1991

Taking pictures was not allowed. They followed the word of God as it is written;

"But when you give to the needy, do not let your left hand know what your right hand is doing, so that your giving may be in secret. Then your Father, who sees what is done in secret, will reward you" (Matthew 6:3-4).

They did not want to be like the Pharisees, who exaggerated their good deeds and sought the praise of people.

At the center, I met a nun who walked with crutches. She encouraged me over the fact that I came so far to meet the people here. After I came back to Berkeley, I sent a letter to her with a small amount of money and with a prayer that God be with her throughout her life. I started to donate and write letters to an Iranian boy through 'Save the Children', which was a small thing that I can do, as Mother Teresa did.

My Mother

After all the hard things in her life, my mother had a stroke while I was at Berkeley. She desperately wanted to see me. She made a good recovery, and she could walk by herself. She came with my father and two brothers to Berkeley for a month before my graduation. My heart was broken to see her face with deep wrinkles and her legs and arms weakened by the stroke. I grasped her rough hands, with which she had done so much hard labor in her life.

She always worried about me who could only walk with crutches. "You look tired. Are you eating properly?" If I cough, she worries again. "Do you have a cold? Or do you have a pain in your lung?"

Whenever I think about her, I cannot help crying. She lived her life in fear and with deep sighs because of my father's drinking habit and violence, yet she took care of six children until she broke down.

I always worried that she might leave the house. My big sisters told Mom to run away from Father. I was around six years old. I could not find Mom in the field, nor in the house. My heart started to beat fast. I looked for her everywhere. I was crawling around in the peach orchard crying in the dirt. She was crouching and cleaning up something at the corner of the orchard, and when she found me crying, she ran to me and hugged me tightly. "My baby, I will never run away, leaving you here behind."

My mother was born in Guapsan, a small village in Chungnam, as a first daughter among two daughters and one brother. The only elder brother died during the Korean War, and they could not find his body. Mom got married by arrangement to my father at the age of twenty. Right after the marriage, my father went to the war as a soldier. She had my first sister, and she took care of seven brothers-in-law in her parent-in-law's house. After my father came back safe from the war, they moved to a village, 'Sambat-ne,' to cultivate a peach orchard and raise animals. My parents did not go to elementary school, and physical labor was their only way to survive.

My mother was small and weak. She ate very little. My father was not happy about it, as she was too weak for heavy field work. She worked until she collapsed. Finally, when I was in middle school, she had a disk operation on her spine.

When I went to college in Seoul, she followed me. She stayed with me until I graduated, helping me with my bag and holding an umbrella for me on rainy days. I asked Mom to go to church. She went to church with an old lady living nearby who was taking care of a grandson alone, and they attended the Sunday service and prayer meeting early in the morning. Maybe that was the happiest and the most peaceful period in her life, with her loving son, away from her husband.

My brothers and father went back to Korea after a week, but Mom stayed with me for a month. I was renting a room with two other graduate students on the first floor of a house. Since three male students were sharing the house, the kitchen and bathroom were very dirty. Mom cleaned the refrigerator by taking out rotten food, and she cleaned the bathtub. I took a walk with Mom along the Marina and we went to San Francisco to have seafood. That was the second happiest moment in her life. She thanked God that she could come to America to see her son who was doing well in his studies. But I swallowed tears while I was driving with Mom, who suffered so much and became half-paralyzed in the end.

"Dear Lord, please give healing to the crushed body of my mom!" But God left her in her condition as it was, and I obeyed his will.

Heeryoung, my wife

I met many good Christians during the six years in the States. I met my wife, the other half of me, also during that time. After a year passed at Berkeley, Yunhee, who was studying in Cologne, whom I knew from Bible study at ESF, sent me a letter. She wrote that she knew a good Christian sister in Cologne and it would be good to exchange letters with her to encourage each other. I wrote a letter to that sister, Heeryoung, a cello student. The letters were pure. They were about faith, the church, studies, friends, and our daily life. While writing these letters, my thoughts became organized, sometimes comforted, sometimes reflective.

Here are some letters that we exchanged:

> *Bright silver sunshine shining through a clear blue sky. Brownish colored silent leaves stirred by wind occasionally. The melody of soft piano sounds waking up a dormant soul in serenity.*
>
> *It is the Sunday morning when Jesus is risen. Yesterday was the end of the semester. I saw two movies in a quiet movie theater. One is "Urga (Close to Eden)," the other is "Of Mice and Men."*
>
> *The first movie is about a Mongolian family who descended from Genghis Khan, who lived in a vast grass field appreciating nature humbly. The movie was directed by Nikita Mikhalkov. It depicts the conflict between tradition and civilization as seen through the eyes of a Russian driver under the Soviet revolution. Now on the grass field, many factories are built, and the grass field became a lost paradise.*
>
> *The second one is about the migration of two people from farm to farm at the beginning of American history. One man*

is a bit mentally retarded, so his friend must take care of him.

This strong and big man likes rats, puppies, and rabbits. Even though people make fun of him, to his friend Gorge, he is a genuine friend sharing life together. But he has to die because this world did not accept him as an equal human being.

The movie depicts loneliness, love, and meanness of human-beings.

Soon after, I will go to church with young brothers in Christ. I believe that only Jesus can cure our loneliness, sorrow, isolation and all the evilness of our society and civilization.

Around Christmas time, I always remember my childhood. I have the impression that sorrow and hope cross each other in the darkness. When I think about my friends abandoned in the shadow of this world, my heart aches, but if I think about the baby Jesus disarmed of everything, born in this land, it gives me hope and strength. Maybe tears and joy are coexisting gifts from God.

Sister, on Christmas, have a good fellowship in the church and praise our Jesus with your cello expressing your soul. Express our friend Jesus who came in a manger with your gesture of life. I will try my best also. I pray that your soul will be deepened and cleansed in Christ in 1993.

Your brother in Christ

Next year, after I was ill in bed for a few days, I wrote a letter as follows:

What do you think about on such a late night?

Have you ever stayed awake the whole night by looking at the shooting stars in the dark, and you feel suddenly everything is awkward?

Nameless trees on the small road that you used to walk for several years, familiar-looking neighbors that you cross paths with often, clearly remembered faces from your hometown in your memory, the face of your mother that you want to see with an aching heart. All these things become a moonlight which lights up your bed, and you cannot go to sleep; do you have such nights?

The face in the mirror that you looked at while brushing your teeth looks so unfamiliar to you. Sometimes do you feel that the clouds that you saw with sleepy eyes under the warm spring sunshine in a blue sky, and the clouds you see now in the foreign sky sitting at the desk, look different?

Have you ever been lying in bed in despair looking at the ceiling with an uncontrollable shaky mind so that you don't have a strength to move even your fingers?

Ah! Do you have those days when living in this world pushes down a heavy weight on your shoulders? Tonight is such a night to me. A day when I wanted to fly up in the air, wanted to be free completely.

How have you been? There it must be April when the green is thriving. The trees and flowers with aliveness, they are silent, but they have the smell of life.

Like those who have life and love in their heart.

One day I find myself too fragile even though I look strong. Then I kneel down before God in prayer. The solitude of my soul, conversation with God, revitalization of soul; these cycles would repeat in my life.

Sister Heeryoung, please take good care of yourself. Do not become weak like me. I pray that tomorrow morning my soul will wake up under the golden sunshine and I send God's love to you.

Inkang.

It took about two weeks for a letter to be delivered to Germany, and after another two weeks, a letter from Heeryoung arrived. She was humble and pure:

I got your letter with joy. It is always encouraging and soothing. Now it is a feast period here. There are many people with different masks on the street. I feel lonelier maybe because I am a foreigner.

... these days in the church I remember what you said in your letter. The phrase that I should praise God with my soul gives me strength. But I wonder what kind of things I can do and wonder if I am that helpful to others at all. I try my best to live like a Christian remembering your words. I always confess that I am so small. It is not humbleness, but I say it as it is.

Please pray for me that I may live my life with strength and courage. Without any specific reason, I am frustrated these days. I don't have the courage to challenge life.

Brother Inkang! Stay healthy. God, who took care of you until now, will be with you today, tomorrow and forever. Goodbye.

From Heeryoung Park.

We wrote letters for five years. Whether there were joyful or difficult moments, we sent letters containing prayers and thoughts to encourage each other. As God loved me unconditionally, I thought I can love her even though I hadn't seen her yet. We promised to see each other in Paris around Christmas when I went to some conference in Paris. Yunhee was living in Paris at that time.

Heeryong came to Paris with several friends. Her first impression was warm and humorous. She treated me naturally regardless of my physical condition. We went up to the Eiffel Tower and walked along the Champs-Élysées. I was almost sure that Heeryoung was my other half that God prepared for me, or maybe I hoped that was true. I promised her that I would go to Cologne when I returned to Paris. There is a direct train from Gare du Nord to Cologne. She nodded. Later, Heeryoung told me a story. My letters to Heeryoung were famous among her friends and were passed around among them.

When she came to Paris to meet me, an elder gentleman came with her to judge me. He was shocked to see my severe disability at first.

"I am against this relationship."

But after we had dinner and conversations together, he changed his mind.

"I am totally for this marriage!"

After I came back to Berkeley, my letters to Heeryoung got longer and longer, telling about my childhood, my family background and everything without hiding anything. I wrote a letter like:

> *I learned what sacrifice means through the life of my mother who endured everything as most Korean women did at that time. When I remember my mother wiping away sweat with a sigh under the scorching sun of midday, it makes me cry. I like a woman who has her own thoughts and her own dreams, because I think no woman should live her life like my mother did. I hope that my wife will enjoy her life and fulfill her dream equally as man has his own right and his own attitude about his life... I will write to you soon again. Please try the song that I sent you.*
>
> *Love*

I had opportunities to attend conferences in Paris since 1995. I also stayed two months at the Henri Poincaré Institute. Whenever I went to Paris, I also went to Cologne to visit Heeryoung. The midnight train from Gare du Nord would arrive in Cologne at seven the next morning. When I looked out the window half-sleepy, she was waiting at the station waving her hands at me.

We had Schweinshaxe and drank Kölsch made in the brewery in Cologne. A spaghetti restaurant, a paella restaurant, bakeries, and pretty German shops sparkled through the night lights. We walked along the lake at Köln University, weaving through families and ducks on the grass and got to know each other more deeply.

She played 'Emperor' for me, the one that I used to listen to at the Marina while watching the sunsets over San Francisco Bay. She always put others first. She spent much of her time with friends that needed her, rather than with her studies and her cello. She cooked for them, looked for housing for them, and took them to the hospital when they were sick, even though she had a test the next day. I liked her a lot since she humbly approached people first. She was always surrounded by people. I am used to a life alone, but she is used to a life together. She didn't stop caring for people, even though many problems cropped up as a result of taking care of them. She walked in somebody else's shoes, even when it was necessary to be selfish.

She got a diploma from Maastricht, but she began cello quite late in high school. During her studies, to earn stipends, she worked in a restaurant and in a printing shop. After I visited her in Cologne, I learned how difficult her financial situation was. On the second floor where she lived, there were several rooms arranged like a dormitory. Korean, Taiwanese and American students shared a bathroom and a kitchen. Heeryoung served in a church as a teacher for children and played cello for a choir.

When we met in Paris again, we walked all day long. From Picasso Museum to Jardin du Luxembourg, Cathedral Notre Dame and Louvre Museum, I don't remember a day that I walked that much. We rode in a boat on the Seine, looking at street vendors and small churches, and we talked and ate in restaurants. In a flower shop, I bought a rose for Heeryoung. At that time, my French was not fluent enough, and it was difficult to communicate with the shop owner. If I asked a question in English, he answered back in French.

Some people marry in consideration of family background, diploma, and appearance, but I never did. A Christian should be against the stream of the world and bold enough to surpass it. We are covered with flaws, but we can embrace each other as we are. Definitely, man and wife can do so. Even though we start love out of chemical emotion, to complete love, we need to practice a lot of patience. We have to learn to love the partner in his or her shoes. In the name of love, even in the name of truth and God, we sometimes imprison a person that we claim to love.

Through my relationship with Heeryoung, I learned to appreciate the beauty of waiting, the beauty of missing someone, and the beauty of love just because that person lives on the same planet. I listened to the tape that she recorded for me and felt the aching

Beautiful Hidden Flowers

My wife, Heeryoung in Cologne in 1995

beauty of life: *Nocturne* by Tchaikovsky, *Kol Nidrei* by Max Bruch, *Cello Concerto* by Elgar, *Arpeggione Sonata* by Schubert. I spent the last days at Berkeley lying on the grass in Emeryville, reading books, studying math and writing letters to Heeryoung. I spent the lovely days that God permitted even though I was sometimes unbearably lonely and down. I wrote a long letter to Heeryoung. That was to ask her to marry me and to walk with her for the rest of my life.

8

Joy Formula

And I made a rural pen,
And I stain'd the water clear,
And I wrote my happy songs Every child may joy to hear.
(William Blake, *Songs of Innocence*)

Joy Formula

During the last year at Berkeley, I attended GCF (Graduate Christian Fellowship) which belongs to IVF. With Dan, a chemist who went to China for a few years after graduation, John, a statistician, a seminary student from Hawaii, and a student from the Poly Sci department who is a professor at USC now, we all gathered together. I only served jasmine and blackberry tea when we had gatherings at my place, but we studied the Bible together and prayed for each other. Through various Christian communities, I came to know that our Christian life should be joyful. Jesus said, "I have told you this so that my joy may be in you and that your joy may be complete" (John 15:11).

Keeping God's commands should be joyful. Without joy, only legalistic, passive, lifeless belief will remain.

In middle school, several guys made fun of me with primitive language. When I walked with crutches wearing braces, everyone looked at me, some with contempt, some with curiosity, some with pity. Whatever it was, I felt insulted. To stay calm, I needed to ignore them. I practiced numbness so as not to be hurt by people. It was like being in hot water and then telling yourself it is not hot. Even though I endured it, my flesh was burned, and the scars remain. After a while, more scars formed over the scars until I felt numb; my heart had become hardened, and the smile disappeared from my face.

At university, I read the verses in the Bible where Jesus received many insults from Roman soldiers, just as I had received insults. Herod made Jesus a public scorn, Pharisees and Scribes condemned him, Roman soldiers slapped and spit in his face and made fun of him. Even on the cross, Jesus was scorned by a robber and by passersby. But Jesus prayed to God, which was a great shock to me. Jesus said, "Father, forgive them, for they do not know what they are doing" (Luke 23:34).

It was a complete forgiveness, a complete love!

How is this possible? This is not the prayer that one can do just before death in the unimaginable pain caused by a torn body! Only an infinite love makes this possible. Indeed, a finite human being will never understand the word 'infinite,' nor be able to put it into practice. But it is natural to God, who exists in an infinite dimension. Infinite love and infinite forgiveness are God's words. Even though Jesus was embodied in human flesh, such an infinite love was possible because he became one with God through his obedience.

At the moment I was grafted to God, I forgave my father, the middle school guys and all the people who hurt me. After that, the smile came back. The clogged spring of joy burst out. Like Habakkuk, I, like many human beings, despair when we looked at the evil things in this world. Not just the evil in the world but the evil inside me also. I confess like Paul: "What a wretched man I am! Who will rescue me from this body that is subject to death?" (Romans 7:24).

But no matter how big the sin and the arrogance are, they are finite. I have hope in the fact that the evil in this world is finite. I have greater hope that the finite things divided by the infinite God's love is zero. What a wonderful twist this is!

That is the evidence that the only thing which can change this world into a flawless, sinless place is the infinite God's love.

I found a mathematical formula that I learned from the Bible, 'Joy Formula.'

Graduation ceremony for doctoral degree in 1996

Jesus said in the Upper Room:

"I have told you this so that my joy may be in you and that your joy may be complete. My command is this: Love each other as I have loved you" (John 15:11-12).

To put it in a math formula, let joy be a function depending on a variable y.

Then *Joy (y) = y (God's love)$^{sign\ of\ y}$*.

In the above equation, the sign of y is ±1. A negative thing such as sin gets −1 and a positive thing such as love gets +1. For example:

Joy= (sin) (God's love)$^{-1}$ = 0.

Joy= (faith, love each other) (God's love)^{1} = ∞.

In other words, if a sinner, injustice or crime meets infinite God's love, the sinner becomes without sin and forgiven after divided by the infinite God's love; injustice will be gone, and the sin will disappear. If the infinite God's love meets a people and a society that practice loving each other in faith, those people will have infinite joy and peace that this world cannot take away, and the kingdom of God, the paradise, will come.

God's infinite love is like a Dirac Delta function. It is a distribution whose total integral is 1 over the real line, whose value at the origin is infinite and 0 otherwise. If God's love encounters the sin anywhere except at the origin, it makes the sin 0, and if God's love encounters a beautiful God's community at the origin, it fills up the community with infinite joy.

If we love each other in church, our joy becomes infinite. Hence, God's community is located at the origin. The fact that the total integral of love is 1 is also graceful.

God's love is for everyone. If someone accepts his love, he will reach the infinite joy, salvation, but if someone rejects his love, God's love will not affect him. Hence the joy is zero.

I shared God's love with the brothers in GCF, and my joy became infinite.

In May 1996, after six years of Berkeley life, I finally got my doctoral degree. I was weak, but God is strong and almighty. I prepared for my return to Korea, expecting his guidance in the next step of my life.

A professor holding a concert

I became a professor at KAIST (Korea Advanced Institute of Science and Technology) after I returned to Korea. The professors there welcomed me, considering my potential for future discoveries, especially Professor Myoung, who was a big help. He has since passed away, but I truly thank him for his kindness. He exerted all his effort to found an institute for pure science like KIAS (Korea Institute for Advanced Study).

At that time, a TV series, 'KAIST,' was popular. Thanks to that series, KAIST was known as a university for science geniuses. In fact, there are many geniuses in KAIST. Most of the students

studied until 3 or 4 am and then they slept very late in the morning. They stayed in the office most of the time, and the campus was very empty. They are trained in math and science from an early age. Even though they are smart, they are very stubborn and have a strong pride. Some of them are weird and have problems in relationships with others.

If one stays alone too long, his soul and mind will develop some problems. He will not get along well with others, even in marriage and in the workplace. Even the campus festival is science oriented. This atmosphere was definitely not healthy for students. Indeed, some of them became hackers, or indulged in drinking or Internet games. I did something. First, I organized 'Math and music night' for my students. On the second floor of the cafeteria at seven o'clock on Saturday, I held a small concert for piano, violin, flute, guitar, and singing. I invited some professors to play guitar. The feedback was positive. At the year-end party, we were invited again.

The transition from a student to a professor was awkward at first. But as I did so far, I listened to the students, gave them advice about their life and future, and tried to be an open-minded professor. My advisor, Andrew Casson, was a world-famous mathematician, but he put a lot of effort into the education of students. Even before something as simple as the calculus class, he wrote down the materials he had to cover during the class.

I learned from him how a scholar and a professor should live. I tried my best to teach students with patience and lead them to have the right attitude toward their studies and academia.

Several students that I taught in KAIST continued their studies at good universities in the States and became important personas in several areas. One of them even became a vice president at Morgan Stanley. But there are also several students who haven't found their way out yet. I hope they can figure out their way soon. That is the teacher's mind.

Near my house, there was a Baptist church where Pastor Ahn Isook and Kim Dongmyoung have ministered. Pastor Ahn wrote a moving book entitled, 'I Will Die if I Need To.' I had a good fellowship in that church. Each member of the congregation tried to live their life by applying their faith to a concrete situation. Some did prison ministry, and some invited children without parents to their homes once every two weeks. Once someone is enrolled in the church, they are taught the Bible from the basics. They tried to live out the words, 'The power of the gospel is not in words but in practice.'

After I had a job and a good church to attend, I needed to deal with the marriage issue. Heeryoung came back to Korea shortly after I arrived, and she had many thoughts. She worked as a first cellist of the Changwon orchestra. Some say that love only matters; others say that marriage is reality. When her parents visited her, they went to Young Frau together. She said, "From high above, the things on the ground look small. Our life is the same. Everything will pass away fast."

Her parents left the decision to her.

"If you will not regret and will be responsible for your decision, we will respect your decision."

Traveling with Heeryoung after marriage in 1998

Since her brother knew me from ESF, he was at my side. Heeryoung's grandmother also was happy about our marriage after she saw me. She thought that I had sparkling eyes. We got married surrounded by friends and families in the blessings of God. Teacher Choi, my elementary teacher, and Jeonwha, my rehabilitation center friend, came to Changwon to celebrate the wedding.

We went to Gyoungju for our honeymoon.

After getting married, we traveled together whenever there were opportunities. We went to a small island near Marseille. There was a serene small pond with mixed colors of blue, red, and green. I wanted to come back after my children grew up. We had bouillabaisse and traveled along the Mediterranean Sea to Morocco in a train. We took a Talgo to Barcelona. The Talgo runs between France and Spain, but when it enters into Spain, its wheels change width, according to the Spain railway. We saw *Sagrada Familia* by Gaudi in Barcelona. On the front wall, I saw the carving of Peter, who was wailing after he denied Jesus three times. It seemed to depict the weakness of human beings and the greatness of God's love, which embraces our weakness.

After that, we traveled to southern Germany. We crossed the snow-covered land in a slow train. We went up to Neuschwanstein Schloss in a chariot. We spent a night in a nearby pension. The owner lady was big and looked scary, but she was kind. She packed boiled eggs for us so that we could have them on the train. We tapped the eggs against the window of a train to crack the shell, and in the process, we found a raw egg, which made us laugh happily.

When I was young, I stayed home all day long. Only when my mom or sisters carried me on their back, could I go to a place like a road leading to a village. I saw yellow flowers on the road swaying to and fro in the breeze when my mom carried me on her back to the hospital. Sometimes I asked Mom to pluck the flowers for me. When I read 'Le Petit Prince,' I dreamed about traveling around the world, the countries beyond the mountain under the sky that I saw from the peach orchard. Twenty years later, my dream came true. I can travel the world and even do it together with my wife.

Three things that I ask myself

Three years after I came to KAIST, I moved to Seoul National University. I did not want to do it in the beginning, but professors kept phoning me and sending me emails to come to SNU.

Leaving a quiet, clean Daejon, and going to noisy, polluted, and expensive Seoul did not look attractive. But I finally decided to go since there are many things to do on campus that I used to struggle to do when I was a university student. Beginning in the fall semester of the year 2000, I started lecturing in the math department. I led a Bible study in my office with students who wanted to study the Bible. I wanted to give hope to some students who might struggle as I did at university, where I was in despair, but found God and learned to love and forgive people.

I taught students to be like Daniel, who was determined before God. Whatever situations may come up, one has to have a faith which can relativize everything before the absolute God. Furthermore, we discussed God's presence in us, loving and serving the community in the oneness of Jesus Christ, and having a concrete practice for our faith. University life is a mixture of hope and despair. It is extremely important to help the students to organize their value system by the logos of words and to plan their future in relation to God.

The campus appeared peaceful. In SNU's Acropolis, which used to be filled with tear bombs, demonstrators, police, and shouting, some of the students walking by are much taller and more handsome than we. Will they ever know the shouting, suffering, and agony that my generation went through for a better future on the stairs of the Acropolis? Probably, in the same way, we do not know the sad history, the sweat, the blood and tears that our father's generation endured. Now, instead of such big goals to change the world into a better place, this new generation has individualism, successfulness, and romanticism. But in this new paradigm, again, they are astray, over-competing, hurt and isolated. They are not confident about their future at all.

I met a student at a parking lot for the handicapped who was in a wheelchair. His mother sometimes cleaned my car while she was waiting for her son. She asked me one day, "How could my son be like you, professor?"

I replied, smiling, "Send him abroad for study by himself."

She worried about sending him alone. Whether healthy or disabled, if he cannot be independent, he will never be successful in life. Man does not step forward if he has a space to step back. If he has that space, it is a blessing but a disaster at the same time.

What I learned from teaching the students at SNU is that the total amount of unhappiness is not changing. Now, it seems that most people have a better life than in the past during poverty, war, and tyranny; however, they are not striving for better, and the indifference toward God is increasing. Maybe this age needs more gospel than ever before. They have to know who created us, after which they have to know the purpose of life, and after that, they have to be confident about how they should live. People talk about 'the call' these days. But the meaning seems to be diminished to only 'job searching.' The call means a life determined for God. The ultimate goal of the call is to be more like Jesus. We can change our jobs. But what I am cannot be changed easily. To be better people, we need to practice holiness, abstinence from sin and greediness, and to be faithful to God for which we are called.

I ask three things every day.

The first is 'holiness.'

The book of Daniel guided me through my life. According to Daniel's decision not to take any king's food, I abstained from drinking, smoking, coffee and love affairs during my days at the university. I concentrated only on study and church life. It could become very legalistic, but I wanted to learn from Daniel's pure heart; as his name suggests, 'God is the only judge.' Whenever I become weak in faith, I read Daniel Chapter 6:

> *"Now when Daniel knew that the writing was signed, he went home. And in his upper room, with his windows open toward Jerusalem, he knelt down on his knees three times that day, and prayed and gave thanks before his God, as was his custom since early days"* (Daniel 6:10).

At last, he was thrown into the den of lions, but God kept him safe from the lions. His holiness defeated the evil of this world. For God's supernatural power to intervene in our lives, our daily lives should be holy. Because of this, I practice holiness every day.

The next thing I ask for myself is purity. The governors and satraps who accused Daniel could not find any charge or fault except that he worshiped God.

In the days of Daniel and even in these days, if evil people know that we are Christians, they will try to find charges and faults against us. They condemn us and say that we are not holy enough, not enough like Jesus. If they cannot find any charge against us except our faith in God, what a glorious charge it is! Disappointingly, the credibility of Protestants is much lower than that of Buddhists and the Catholic Church, according to a recent poll in Korea. How shameful this is. I must myself repent. No matter how faithful we look, if we have an ethical problem, we are not genuine Christians. The deed of purity is a moral life, and this is a daily sacrifice for Christians. We really have to take ethical purity seriously. The fate of the church depends on this.

Lastly, I have to ask myself every day whether I did my best with the things that God entrusted me with. Daniel had wisdom. The king, Belshazzar, said:

> *"I have heard of you, that the Spirit of God is in you, and that light and understanding and excellent wisdom are found in you" (Daniel 5:14).*

If young Christians put their effort and time in faith and study, they will excel in everything. A dream without ability is unrealizable. In society, Christians should be responsible and capable with what they have to do. Especially those who want to be scholars; they have to improve their ability to be used for a good purpose.

I had many opportunities to meet famous people in the math world. Some of these people are very obnoxious. They attack speakers openly during seminars. But if they are big shots, such things are tacitly accepted, and sometimes they are praised as brilliance. Such acts make for gossip over dinner, but they are not pleasant at all. Some scholars are both intelligent and mature. If being successful is the scholar's only goal, he would not care about maturity nor about relationships with others. But being immature and obnoxious cannot be justified by being famous and brilliant.

I am a small person. I suffered from illness, discrimination, and poverty as a lowborn person. I have many smart peers. Sometimes I feel too small when I compare myself to them. But I learned from God to be content with what I have. I do things to the best of my abilities, and I serve others with what I have. I study math as well as I can, but I am not obsessed with being successful. My calling from God is to be a scholar who is pious and moral, and who does his best in the study of math, and who proclaims the gospel in any circumstance. Even though we are sinful, we have a calling to be mature to the measure of Jesus Christ. Following the path of Jesus, who was poor but rich in spirit, who had hope in the midst of suffering, who gave everything to us even if he was in need, is our calling from God.

Light steps of a scholar

The policy for education in Korea is very short-sighted. We need two tracks at the same time. One track is to educate elite students, and the other is to educate all other people. These two must be cooperative yet separate. But in our country, these two policies

Fila Basic Science Award in 2016

are confused. Our society classifies students into two groups: those of us who attend prestigious universities, and those who don't. Anyone has a right to be happy in accordance with his ability and aptitude. But it is not allowed here.

The same confusion occurs in academia. Rather than opening

up a new, creative field, we mimic what we have learned from other countries and from other universities. To evaluate professors, the government counts the number of our publications regardless of their quality. Professors are under great pressure for promotion, to teach, and to perform administrative duties. To meet the promotion requirement, they stay in their offices until very late, but overworking does not give creativity. In fields like mathematics, we need several years to resolve just one problem. Mathematicians cannot produce papers as professors in engineering do. The government always talks about the Nobel Prize or the Fields medal. But to have such prizes, the potential, the atmosphere and long periods of investment need to be present. Such prizes come naturally and unexpectedly. The government should plan for these things in a course of one hundred years, not just in a five-year period.

My advisor, Casson, never pushed me. I wouldn't see him for six months if I had no ideas about the problem that I was working on. But he waited until I found something by myself. I became free from competition and low self-esteem as I learned the attitude of a scholar who does not just mimic others. No matter how shabby it seems to look, a scholar should build his own house.

While I was viewing the paintings of Vincent van Gogh, I read a collection of letters between him and his brother Theo. He loved painting even though he was poor and lonely all through his life. While other painters were drawing portraits to make money, he drew a wilderness, a field where rough-handed farmers were sweating, and a golden field where ravens were flying at sunset. He suffered from delusion after writing poems on canvas by the color of his own soul. He wrote on the white wall with the blood of his fingers, "My soul is whole."

Even though no one recognized him, he was a genuine artist who struggled to create his own world to capture his mad passion on canvas. A scholarly way is not different from the road of an artist.

The wise man, Solomon, wrote in Proverbs 30:7-9:

"Two things I ask of you, Lord; do not refuse me before I die:

Keep falsehood and lies far from me; give me neither poverty nor riches, but give me only my daily bread.

Otherwise, I may have too much and disown you and say, 'Who is the Lord?' Or I may become poor and steal, and so dishonor the name of my God."

I also want to have this attitude about life. I managed to be free from people's judgment and the bad structure of society and to be calm before the swamp of life and death, maybe because I went through a tough life and God gave me true freedom.

I never wanted to be on the top of the pyramid and to be recognized by people, because if I were in such a whirlpool of competition, my soul would have been destroyed. The desire to be on the top is the most dreadful sin, which eats away our life. Luckily and gratefully, I was awarded the 'Young Scientist Award' in 2007 and the 'FILA Basic Science Award' in 2016 for the recognition of my research on geometry and topology in Korea. I regard this as an encouraging gift from God. I decided to be more faithful to what I am doing, to be a scholar with a solid foundation.

The next year, 2008, I left Seoul National University and moved to KIAS (Korea Institute for Advanced Study). KIAS was founded in 1996 and modeled after IAS in Princeton. This is the only place in Korea that one can dedicate his whole time to research without teaching and administrative duty. Many people discouraged me when I said that I am moving to KIAS. But I didn't want to settle down complacently in the present. I wanted to challenge myself. If one stays in one place too long, everything becomes routine, and the spirit to challenge disappears.

The other reason to move to KIAS was my physical condition. It was extremely difficult for me to give lectures because writing on a blackboard for several hours a day left me drenched in sweat. I decided to dedicate my time more to mathematics itself without the restrictions that a civil worker has in Korea. That was a decision to take the light step of a scholar to dedicate more to research, free from any bondage that holds me back.

Gunwoo and Harin along Rhine River in 2009

9

God Makes Me Smile

You turned my wailing into dancing; you removed my sackcloth and clothed me with joy, that my heart may sing your praises and not be silent.

Lord my God, I will praise you forever (Psalm 30: 11-12).

Cosmo boy and summer giraffe mademoiselle

I have a son and a daughter. They run and play all day long with healthy legs. We have to live on the ground floor in the apartment building as not to disturb the people downstairs.

Teacher Choi named my son Gunwoo 'Builder of the Universe', and my daughter Harin 'Summer Giraffe.' My boy and girl like to play, and they eat well.

Gunwoo was a little brat when he was young. He is very sportive, even though he has a shy face with long eyelashes. He likes making things, experimenting, and drawing things in detail. He wants to be a person who invents machines and chemical materials. He messes up the whole house with soap, vinegar, milk, paint, and flour all mixed together to make a magical potion. He draws very detailed objects like a future city, a factory, and construction sites. We cannot believe that a child can draw such detailed pictures. Many foreign children envy him. Teachers also frequently encourage him to develop his artistic talent. My wish is that he will be a man with a warm heart and a pure soul, whatever he does in the future. I used to sing a song to Gunwoo since he was in my wife's belly. I heard this song in a church at Rennes at a baptizing ceremony.

> "Seigneur dirige et santifie.
> Toute la vie de ses enfants.
> Que ta lumière sur leur carrière brillant tout temps
> Que sous ta garde et sous tes ailes ils soit fiedèle et confident."

My daughter, Harin—when she sleeps, she looks like an angel. It reminds me of the phrase that I learned at Berkeley "Duerme como los ángeles."

Her soft, chubby cheeks make me peaceful. Content with milk, and joyful as if she had the whole world when we give her a loving look. Maybe that is why Jesus said that the kingdom of heaven belongs to children, the place where people, who are happy with God's loving look, could go. Harin is calm and patient, much different from Gunwoo. I pray that they become a brother and a sister who can rely on each other, and who are good examples to each other.

I cannot help my wife with house chores. I can wash dishes, but I cannot change light bulbs, cannot nail things to the wall. I cannot hold a baby in my arms to put him to sleep. I cannot push carts in a shopping mall. Heeryoung does a lot of work to take care of the children. Instead, I read books before they go to sleep and help them with their studies. I take them to museums and to concerts. I play ping-pong with Gunwoo, and we go to a swimming pool together.

Once I played soccer with small children in a park in Bonn. Gunwoo and I played against two German children. I was a keeper. Since I have four legs, I blocked many shots, but we were beaten by 10-2. After the game, they told me that they played on a youth team. I noticed that they played very well indeed.

Sometimes my children say, "If Dad can walk...."

Once, we encountered a very dangerous situation on the beach in Malaga. I was sitting on the beach watching Gunwoo playing with a bucket. Suddenly, he disappeared from my sight, and we found that he was drowning. I could not run to him, and I shouted, "Help, help, my son is drowning!" A young man who was swimming in the ocean took Gunwoo out of the water. What a dreadful experience it was! After that, I decided to learn swimming, and now I can swim in the ocean.

Since the time with children passes away quickly, I try to play with them as much as I can. I want to be a father who can talk to Gunwoo like a friend and will want to share everything with him, but it is not easy. Gunwoo is a bit hot-tempered. When he was young, he often fought with peers. One day, a parent of a child who fought with Gunwoo came to my house. I reconciled both children after I heard what happened. He has to discipline himself to control his temper. Usually, we talk about it after such things happened to help him discern what is wrong and what is right.

After Gunwoo started elementary school, he began goofing off with me.

"Gunwoo, shall we recite multiplication table?"

"Why should we?"

"For example, if you buy five soaps, and know the price of soap, you can know the price of five without adding them."

"I can use a calculator."

"...."

"Gunwoo, let's study English."

"Why should we study English?"

"If you go to a country where people speak English, then you have to speak English to buy things, to give lectures and to communicate with them."

"They can learn Korean, instead."

"If they come to Korea, they learn Korean, but if we go there, we have to speak their language."

"Dad, I will hire an interpreter."

"....."

While I was thinking about what to do with him, he had already disappeared to play with friends. I want to give many things to my children. I want to give them all I have, wisdom, money, opportunities and even my life. But Gunwoo does not know what is good nor even care about it. Now I can understand the mind of God. He gave us everything, even his only begotten son. But, we don't even care about it. I realized that it is very difficult to be a good parent.

I cannot believe that I have a wife and two children. I have a house and work. I was destined to be a beggar on the street. I used to crawl on the ground.

The unimaginable blessings of God. I thank my family every day whenever I see them.

Several years ago, I went to Berkeley with my family to attend a program at MSRI. During this visit, I met Chulhyun, who is now a professor at Hayward State University. I used to give him a ride and took care of him with many things. Now he is serving on a campus ministry team at Berkeley. At his request, I delivered a sermon to share who God is to me, and how God transformed the earthly things to heavenly things in my life.

I went with my family to the place where I used to walk, used to study, and used to cry and laugh. I walked on the Marina with my family where I used to walk alone. The sparkling golden San Francisco Bay looked prettier than a Mozart's piano sonata.

It was Heeryong's birthday. We went to San Francisco to have an early dinner at Cliff House, and then we walked along the beach. The flow of tides painted beautiful stripes on the beach. I thanked God that we had already lived eight years together as man and wife. As parents, as a teacher in the school, as church members, we will live our life together. How merciful God is for giving me a loving companion and friend on the journey of my life. We took

At Cliff House in San Francisco in 2007

a family picture against the sun going down beyond the ocean. I am sure that it is not easy for her to live with me. Her face, with a sprinkling of gray hair, shone like an angel reflecting the crimson sunset, which contains every moment from when we wrote letters to each other until the moment that we are standing together here.

Tomorrow is the first picnic day for Harin. Every day she packed one thing for the picnic. One day, orange juice. One day snacks. I am watching how happy she is.

Even though I never went to a school picnic during my childhood, I am happy just by looking at her. Our God in heaven should be happy looking at us if we are happy on earth.

Teaching math to Gunwoo

In the second grade, Gunwoo took his first midterm. He had to do multiplication. He played all during summer vacation, and he didn't memorize the multiplication table, which made it difficult for him at the beginning of the fall semester. But the teacher forced him to memorize it, which he barely did. In the beginning, he could not memorize multiples of three. Since he repeated it so many times, Harin, who was listening to what he was reciting, suddenly said 7 times 8 is 56. It made us laugh. Just before the exam, I asked him to solve some math problems, but he could not remember the table. I asked him, what is 7 times 8? He couldn't do it. After a few weeks, he had completely forgotten. My father, who had not even entered elementary school, could calculate in his head the price of peach boxes just by looking at them. How come Gunwoo could not even memorize the multiplication tables?

I made him memorize multiples of 2, 3 and 4. The multiples of 5 are easy. 5, 10, 15, and so on. And I taught him how to do multiples of 6, 7, 8, 9—so-called 'African math.' It is intended to do multiples greater than 6 using the fingers, on the condition that one can do up to 5 already.

I taught him that 6×2, 6×3, 6×4, 6×5 are ok since he knows already the multiples of 2, 3, 4, 5 (commutativity). Now for 6×6. With the left hand, only one finger is stretched out, and the other 4 fingers are folded to indicate 6. The same with the right hand. Each spread finger on the left and right hands counts 10. Folded fingers each count 1. Hence, two spread fingers count 20. Now with 4 folded fingers on the left hand, 4 folded fingers on the right hand, we multiply them together: 4×4=16.

Then 20+16=36. That is the way to do 6×6. Let's do it one more time with 7×8. Now you know on the left hand, 2 spread fingers and 3 folded fingers. On the right hand, 3 spread fingers and 2 folded fingers. Hence 20+30+ 3×2=56!

"Wow, it's magic!"

Gunwoo practiced several times and built up some confidence. He was happy that he did not need to memorize the table after the multiples of 5. Next week, he took the test, and it went OK. He blew his first problem; on the second problem, he made a mistake with a sign. On the third problem, he could not understand the long sentence about the problem. But he added, "Dad, my friend next to me, he memorizes the whole multiplication table, but his score is worse than mine."

It makes sense because math is not for memorization, but for understanding things logically. It trains in logical thinking.

When we were in France, Gunwoo did the calculation in his head with 10 digits, 1000 digits freely since he is trained in Korea. Teachers were very impressed. But they said, "Please do not teach him ahead of the school's curriculum. He does not pay attention in the class."

They teach slowly in France, but they give problems which measure several abilities together: math, language, analytical thinking, etc. France is famous for mathematicians like Poincaré, Descartes, Pascal, Galois, Fermat, Fourier, Cauchy, Laplace, Legendre, Grothendieck, and many others too numerous to name.

Somehow, I am not as good at calculation as I used to be. One day I went to a bank on campus. A female clerk greeted me and smiled at me.

"Are you a math professor?"

"Yes, I am."

"I never imagined. I saw you in a newspaper. I thought that you are a professor of literature or philosophy."

"What made you think that way?"

"You were so bad at calculating the change and the interest rate."

Once, I took a taxi home. After arriving at home, I gave money to a taxi driver and said, "Keep the change."

The taxi driver looked at me ridiculously. "You haven't even paid the fare!"

Maybe because I concentrate on abstract and theoretical math, my ability for calculation is tremendously decreased. Nonetheless, since I have studied math more than 30 years, I can give some advice to children about how to do math.

First, never try to memorize math. One has to understand math.

Second, Study little by little every day. Crash study doesn't work very well for math.

Third, do not pass up a math problem. Study it until you understand it even you go to bed very late.

Fourth, try to solve it by yourself rather than relying on somebody else. A solution you found by yourself will never be forgotten.

Fifth, believe that you are smart. Everything is a matter of confidence.

Sixth, never give up even when your grade is not good. If you work hard for three years, you will be an expert in that field.

Seventh, the more you think, the smarter you will be.

Eighth, look at things mathematically. For example, try to figure out why tiles on the floor are either square or hexagon.

Ninth, make up your own math problems. By doing this, you will understand the concept.

Tenth, teach math to a friend or to a younger sibling. To teach, you must understand the material perfectly.

Live as a cosmopolitan

Our family packs luggage twice a year. Since mathematics is a common language, I can work anywhere in the world. During summer and winter break, I visit math institutes in the world for joint research. We visited America, France, Spain, Sweden, Finland, England, Switzerland, Germany, Belgium, Netherlands, Japan, Singapore, and China.

A woman I know, Mary, invited me to a seminar talk in Liverpool. My advisor, Casson, was once a professor there. She is a very kind person, and we stayed in her house. We toured the town and its museums. Museums are free, and there are places for children inside of them. It was when Gunwoo was very little, and he always tried to touch paintings and sculptures. He had to learn the public rules there.

Japan is our neighboring country, but they are much different from Koreans. They follow codes and rules like Germans. Sometimes, geographical nearness does not imply similarity of culture.

With Mme and M Picinbono and Mme Vuong in Paris in 2003

We went to Singapore at the invitation of Ser. It is a very clean, well-organized, small country, which is a financial and a commercial center in Asia. China has a booming economy and its citizens show off their wealth; many foreign cars such as Mercedes Benzes are riding around in Beijing. But the disorder and pollution were very serious. Wealth alone cannot make a country advanced. After I had a Peking duck in Beijing, I rolled in my bed for the whole night with a stomach ache. I have been amazed at many different cultures and people around the world, but I learned that they are the same human beings created by God.

In 2004, my sabbatical year, we settled down at Bures sur Yvette in the south of Paris. We lived in a house provided by the institute,

IHES. I met a librarian, Francoise, at the institute. She came to my office to bring a book that I asked for and asked me whether I am a Christian. She asked me to read the Bible together with her and shared a story about her life. After she divorced her husband, she brought up her children alone. Her daughter got married to a Muslim, and it made her life difficult.

I went to a Bible study meeting in the village, and I met Picinbono and the Lego family.

Mr. Picinbono was a president of Orsay University. He is a physicist but plays piano very well. They have a sad story. Their beloved daughter Natali died in an avalanche along with her fiancé several weeks before their marriage. At the corner of the living room of their house, there is still a tarnished old photo of her and an old cello that she used to play. They lent Heeryoung that cello, and for the first time in several decades, the cello was played when Heeryoung needed to play in a church. It was probably difficult for them to remember their daughter again, but it was as if they wanted to shake off the bitter memory.

Mr. Picinbono practiced a piece of Beethoven with Heeryoung regularly. Mr. Picinbono gave a sermon in their church from time to time. It was beautiful to see them serving the church, which they had done since they were young. Whenever we go to Paris, they always make us an offer to stay with them. They wait for us to have dinner together, no matter how late we are. From them, I see the love and the face of God who is always waiting for me in heaven preparing a feast. Even when we have to pass through Paris, they ask us to stay over one night with them to relieve our fatigue from the journey. They think of us as their children.

We always stay in Natali's former room. There are many books about philosophy, art, music, history, and culture. I could imagine how many books the French intellectuals read apart from the books related to their specialty. I heard that the renowned mathematician Poincaré was also very knowledgeable about art and literature. That is the education that we call whole-child education.

Madame Beatrice Pincinbono was a history teacher. She cooks such delicious French cuisine for us. My children really like her cooking. She invites so many people to her home, even though her health declined recently. When I stay alone in their house without family, she cooks and does laundry for me as if I am one of her children. She takes care of many nephews, grandchildren, even friends of their children. She puts God's command into practice by her life.

> *"Religion that God our Father accepts as pure and faultless is this: to look after orphans and widows in their distress and to keep oneself from being polluted by the world. You see that a person is considered righteous by what they do and not by faith alone"* (James 1:27, 2:24).

Mr. Lego was a pianist. His wife, Jaqueline, is very much involved in taking care of foreigners and the needy in the church. Their ancestors are from eastern Europe, and recently the bones of their ancestors who were sacrificed by Hitler were found. They serve the same church as the Pincinbono family. I learned that even in France, where the gospel of God seems to have disappeared, there are still remnants of these people.

Another person that we met in the village is Madame Vuong, at whose house we rented a room for six months. She spoke French, German, English and Russian and was one of the intellectuals in that village. She also served people by renting out rooms to foreigners like Russians, Chinese, and Koreans through an association for scientists. Her daughter married a son of Doudy, a French mathematician. Madame Vuong married Mr. Vuong, a Chinese. She has a son of my age. Her daughter-in-law died recently of a brain tumor that she had since marriage. At her last stage of life, Madame Vuong went to her son's house in Paris every day. She tried to stay calm after her daughter-in-law's death. We invited her for dinner to condole with her. I asked her if she would live with her son, but she said, "Even now, when I go to my son's place, I sleep on the sofa. If I sleep in a bedroom, that would mean that I will settle in there. It is his life, and he has to figure it out. I can help him, but I should not intervene in his life. He has to overcome this sadness. Encouraging is more correct than living with him."

Seeing this reminded me of the verse:
"That is why a man leaves his father and mother and is united to his wife, and they become one flesh" (Genesis 2:24).

Marie Jaqueline is a mother of twin sons, Mathew and Julien. She is from Laos and works as a designer. Her husband, Jean-Marc, works in Orange, and he likes Korean movies. They invite me to dinner when I am alone without family. I can understand why the middle class elected Sarkozy as president of France, by having conversations with them. They care about practical things, contrary to most professors. On Wednesdays, Julien and Mathew came to my place to play with Gunwoo and Harin. When we returned to Korea, Marie Jaqueline cried a lot.

When we stayed at MSRI for summer in 2005, Gunwoo met Pierre and Vincent in the preschool. Their family was visiting Berkeley for a year from France. After that, whenever we go to Paris, we drive down to Tours to meet their family. Their parents, Jean and Frederique, are medical professors in the University of Tours. I hope that they keep their friendship until they become adults, and encourage each other even from different continents.

It is through mathematics that I began to develop a relationship with France. When I attended a conference in Switzerland, I met Gilles, Gerard and Francoise. Gerard helped me a lot, like an elder brother. His ancestor is from Italy. He is kind, manly, and very good at math. He visited me several times in Korea, and he likes kimchi, bean soup, and strongly-smelling fermented bean-paste soup, even really strongly-smelling fermented stingray. Wherever he goes, he respects the local culture.

Gilles was a professor at Ecole Polytechnique, one of the best universities in France. Now he is at Paris VI in Jussieu. He is left-wing, married a high school principal, and has two daughters and a son. His hair is like a never-combed bush, but he has a great enthusiasm for mathematics.

Francoise is a female professor at the University of Rennes. I got to know her when she emailed me once asking a math question. She also visited me in Korea a few times, and we became good friends. Now she is happy with a guitarist husband and twin daughters. The twin daughters use chopsticks during their meals, and they call it 'Gunwoo chopsticks.' Whenever I go to Bretagne, I visit her and her family.

In 2006, we spent three months in Madrid working at Complutense University. Raquel, whom I had met at Berkeley by chance, invited me to do joint research with her. Spanish seemed attractive, and I learned it for two months in Madrid. She came to our house with her friends, and we had Korean food, and they danced a Spanish dance. We were invited to her parents' place for paella. We met her whole family. Her parents greeted me, saying that it is an honor for me to visit them from such a far land.

Madrid is a busy city, but it has many beautiful buildings, museums, and squares.

We looked at Goya's paintings and learned about Spanish history. It reached 40 degrees Celsius during the daytime, but by around 10 pm, people got out in the street to have dinner and to enjoy the nightlife until 2-3 am. We visited small cities around Madrid and learned about their culture. Raquel and my family drove together, past sunflower fields and olive trees under the burning Spanish sun, to Portugal to visit Raquel's friend. While driving, we sang together:

> *"Mon coeur t'adore mon Dieu puissant, null n'est comme toi, mon coeur t'adore prince de paix, c'est ce que mon coeur desire, sois glorifié, car tu est ma sainteté, mon coeur t'adore mon Dieu puissant, null n'est comme toi–"*

And a Spanish song that Raquel taught Gunwoo:

> *"Mi barba tiene tres pelos,*
> *Tres pelos tiene mi barba,*
> *Si no tu viera tres pelos,*
> *ya no sería una barba."*

I drove down to the south of Spain to see Mezquita in Cordoba, Alhambra in Granada, a pretty village in Mijas where the houses are all white. I could see the influence of the Moors who conquered Spain for several decades. Even in the language and culture, I could see the Moorish influence.

Every summer, and sometimes for Christmas, we went to Cologne to meet Anna and Kyusuk. Anna was a nurse for forty years, but after a stroke, half of her body was paralyzed. We went there for a week just to be company. She helped out a lot of Korean students and immigrants while she worked in the hospital. Even after the stroke, she prepared foods for Korean nuns staying in a German monastery. Sometimes we even drove to Banneaux in Belgium to deliver food to a Korean nun living in the monastery for many years. The nun was so grateful because she missed Korean food so much. We went to Neumarkt to see Christmas stands, to Stadtwald to take a walk, to see a small zoo in the park, and to mini-golf with children near the lake. Children loved to have German wurst in Neumarkt, and we loved to drink gluhwein in Weihnachtsmarkt. Now Anna and Kyusuk are very old, and they are living in a nursing home.

Starting in 2013, I began to collaborate with Patrick Foulon, who is a director of CIRM in Marseille. Every summer, I drive down to CIRM with my family from Paris to spend two weeks doing research together with Patrick.

The summer afternoon in Marseille is hot. After a big delicious French lunch with Patrick, I usually go to the beach with my family to swim in the Mediterranean Sea. I like the blue sea with the warm Mediterranean sun shining upon me. Patrick and his wife Corrine became good friends with us. Patrick invited us to his house every time we were there. We sang together to the tune of his old guitar, and sometimes I played flute after our big dinners.

In 2013, my family and I spent a year at Goteborg in Sweden. My collaborator, Genkai, invited me to Chalmers University. We had met at a conference in Trieste, Italy. After my talk there, he came up to me and asked several questions. He invited me to Chalmers to give a talk, and we became friends. He still comes to Korea to write mathematical papers together with me.

The Nordic snowy country was quite an experience. During winter, the sun rises around 10 am and sets around 3. I thought it was time to go home in the afternoon, but it was only 4 pm. Goteborg is warmer than Stockholm due to the gulf stream. Yet, it was windy and cold in the winter and snowed a lot. Children wore thick-padded Eskimo overalls. We bought a sleigh to glide down the hills. The weather in the summer is quite pleasant. We used to sit on a balcony to enjoy the fresh summer air, watching passers-by and enjoying the bright summer evening that didn't darken till 11 pm. Sweden has beautiful natural scenery along the sea. The rocky seashores were quite impressive, and the colorful coral reefs and jellyfish were very pretty, but the jellyfish were dangerous when we swam in the cold North Sea.

Our family drove from Paris to Goteborg when we first went to Sweden because my French car had been parked in the garden of

In Goteborg, Sweden in 2013

Madame Vuong's house at Bures sur Yvette. We crossed Germany and then took a big ferry from Kiel to Copenhagen. It was our first time taking such a huge ship on an overnight excursion. We had a nice buffet meal for dinner, and we walked around the boat. Gunwoo tried a slot machine, and luckily, we won some money. As the boat sailed into the deep sea, the sun was setting, and it became windy and cold. After dark, we left the deck and went into our small cabin. It was uncomfortable sleeping in the small, hard bunk beds, but we enjoyed that night trip watching the dark sea out of the round portholes. The next morning, we arrived in Copenhagen, and we crossed Denmark in two hours, bypassing Copenhagen. We crossed a very expensive toll bridge to enter Sweden at Malmo. From there, we arrived at Goteborg. After the boat trip, Heeryoung developed tinnitus, and she is now reluctant to travel by boat.

It was a peaceful stay at Goteborg, full of small family excursions in the city, driving trips to nearby cities, and friendly gatherings with friends. We went to a small Korean church, where we met a Myoungja missionary and a Kwangsub deacon couple, Keunjae's family, and other families. My children liked to meet other Koreans living in a strange land far away from home. Once, I led a Bible study whenever I was there on Sundays.

The children went to ISGR, International School, Goteborg Region. They made international friends in the school, and they liked the food in the cafeteria. Heeryoung also made many international friends while attending many different singing groups, social gatherings, and cooking gatherings. I liked the swimming pool in the city. It had many different kinds of swimming lap lanes, as well as saunas. We dropped by the saunas after swimming to enjoy the heat during that cold winter.

The children's school held an international party once a year. They wore traditional costumes from their home countries, and their parents prepared traditional foods. What I like the most about Sweden is their openness to different people, different cultures, and different languages.

In 2014, I spent a sabbatical year at Stanford University. It brought back all the memories of Berkeley twenty years before. We settled in a small, hilly village, called Belmont, near Stanford. In the apartment complex we lived in, we met wonderful neighbors. Kent and Christine lived a few units down from us. Kent was a pastor in a Methodist church, and Christine was a teacher. They always tried to help us. They wrote letters to the Belmont City Hall requesting ADA ramps be added to the sidewalks near our apartment complex. They gladly proofed the first draft of my manuscript for this book. We attended a nice, small church in the village and met nice people: Micki, Mike, Bob and Belinda, Terry, Elizabeth, and Kristi. Heeryoung and I used to play instruments with the choir. When my family played the hymn 'Thou, My Everlasting Portion'—Heeryoung played cello, Gunwoo and Harin played violins, and I played flute—Belinda came to us in tears and said, "Would you play that song again when I die?"

When Bob and Belinda moved to a nursing home in Redwood City, they gave us a two-hundred-year-old family heritage organ.

With Francoise and Dominique singing chanson together in 2003

A month before my official start at Stanford, I went there to try to find housing for a year. The rent in Palo Alto was extremely high, which forced me to look around the nearby cities. The first day that I went to the international office of Stanford University, I met Hannah, who worked at Bechtel International Center. After I returned to my hotel, I received an email from her. She invited me to a church gathering. Hannah and Hochan, her husband, picked me up to go to Heonsuk's place. That was the first encounter with this community in Palo Alto. My family was happily integrated into that Korean church after our arrival at Stanford. I belonged to the oldest age group, called Kairos, which did ministry to visiting scholars and elderly members. We spent a wonderful time together for a year.

Starting in 2017 and finishing in 2018, Hannah and Hochan turned the garage into a Bible study room, and we gathered at a round table to meditate on the words of God in the cold weather hoping that the garage would be a place for renewing the souls of weary human beings.

I had several occasions to preach to the young adult group on campus, for both Korean and English services, and at several churches in California. I thank God for introducing me to such a wonderful Christian community, even in the States.

I think I will always be cosmopolitan, but wherever I live, I pray that the city becomes a place where the purity of God dwells, a true Jubilee comes, and everything is always new and exciting like the first day.

Let me close this chapter with a 1974 poem by Shel Silverstein:

There is a place where the sidewalk ends
And before the street begins,
And there the grass grows soft and white,
And there the sun burns crimson bright,
And there the moon-bird rests from his flight
To cool in the peppermint wind.
Let us leave this place where the smoke blows black
And the dark street winds and bends.
Past the pits where the asphalt flowers grow
We shall walk with a walk that is measured and slow,
And watch where the chalk-white arrows go
To the place where the sidewalk ends.
Yes we'll walk with a walk that is measured and slow,
And we'll go where the chalk-white arrows go,
For the children, they mark, and the children, they know
The place where the sidewalk ends.

Mission for the francophone

Since I travel to France often, I became familiar with CCMF (Communauté Coreenne des Missions pour la Francophonie). I met David, a French missionary. He had a passion for the gospel, even though he was young. He served in the church in Montreuil where many Muslims live. Most of his congregation were black. A missionary from Portugal started the church to evangelize the local people and to send out missionaries around the world. They tried to live according to the Bible, and I saw the fruits of the Holy Spirit. But David settled down in Marseille and is now heading his own church.

France has a deep Christian background with the likes of John Calvin, but nowadays the reformed church is persecuted by the Catholic Church in many ways. It seemed that Christianity is just part of the culture but not part of their life. The influence of Christians on society seems very weak. On the other hand, I see a lot of Muslim influence in Paris. Many francophonies feel pressured to recover the gospel and to fight against the expansion of Islam. Many missionaries are sent to English speaking areas, but very few are sent to the francophone region. This francophone area is rapidly being invaded by Muslims. It seems to be the last region to be evangelized, and yet is where the gospel should be preached.

There are many Korean churches in France. Even in Paris, there are more than ten Korean churches and more churches around the big cities in the rest of the country. Korean immigration in France does not have a long history compared to the one in the States. Many students study art and music there, but not many influential people settle there except a few world-famous musicians like Myounghoon Jeong and Gunwoo Baik. Pastors there are walking a road that was never taken before. I thank God that they are laboring to establish the kingdom of God, even in France. Before I went to France for a sabbatical year, I led a French Bible study at Sookmyoung Women's University with Ms. Hong, who is an interpreter at Le Cordon Bleu in Seoul. We gathered students from the French department at Sookmyoung, Le Cordon Bleu, and outsiders who were interested in French. We held a gospel feast, inviting the chefs of Le Cordon Bleu. I want to donate some of the proceeds of this book to missionaries to the francophones if it sells well.

My Father

In the fall of 2006, during the trip to Spain, I got an email that my father was in critical condition. He got a hip infection, but as the dosage of antibiotics increased, his kidneys were affected. Since the situation was not getting any better, we transferred him to Seoul National University Hospital. But his health still got worse.

He was born the third child out of nine in a poor family. Two of them had already passed away, and the others had a dramatic life. During Japan's occupation, two elder brothers were conscripted for the war. The eldest brother came back wounded, but the second brother stayed in Japan for various reasons. The youngest brother went to the Vietnam War, and after he came back, he just wandered around the country. My father went to the Korean War for several years but came back safely. Yet his life was more dreadful

With parents and two brothers in Stanford in 1996

fighting against the poverty he fell into. I am not optimistic about the sayings by philosophers that history advances in a positive direction, and that history is the process of thesis, antithesis, and synthesis in a positive direction. This is just abstract nonsense that has nothing to do with my family's history.

Regardless of a person's opinion and will, history will affect him tremendously, and my father got stuck in the whirlpool of Korean history, since he was uneducated, poor and had no social connections. As an uneducated person, he tried to support his family by selling chickens and pigs. He bought a peach orchard with the money saved by my mother and my eldest sister, who collected the empty bullet shells on the military training ground. My parents worked in a peach orchard and grew rice, beans, sesame, potato, sweet potato, strawberry, and tobacco all year round. But we were still poor.

My father was strong and manly. He gave out money to his brothers and to the neighbors even though we didn't have enough for the family. Almost every evening, he got drunk to forget the hard work and his hard life. After that, violence followed. And he screamed to throw me away to the field. Maybe I can understand him now. He must have been afraid. This world is so harsh, even to those who are healthy, but he thought I would be a beggar on the street eventually. He could not see such a thing happen. Such a savage expression could be his love and worry toward me.

After I grew up and accepted God in my heart, I forgave my father. He moved to Seoul during my third year in university. He bought many things from the market very early in the morning. He sold them at the entrance of Kwanak Mountain during the day, and he made puffy rice cakes and fish shape cakes on the street of Shinrim-dong at night. Sometimes officers from city hall controlled the selling on the street without a permit. They would take everything away. Then the next day, my father would go to the city hall and beg and cry to get them back.

He came to Berkeley once with Mom and two brothers. He was on the airplane for the first time. He liked the food on the plane and asked for a meal three times. Since a Korean stewardess refused it, he used body language to try to convince a foreign assistant.

When he was at Berkeley, he talked to anyone on the street 'Korea, Korea'. They just smiled and passed by. If he was born in a rich family and properly educated, he might have become a politician.

After I became a professor at KAIST, my parents moved to Yousung. I met my father for lunch at the traditional market. At lunch in the market, we ate quietly, putting aside all the difficult memories, as a grown-up son and an old father—neither of us showing remorse, and neither asking for a pardon. I cried in my heart as I looked at my father with gray hair and a deeply wrinkled face after his harsh life, a man who struggled with his naked body to support his family by digging the orchard, selling on the street, laboring on the construction site, who never had a rest even for a day!

"Lord, please save this broken soul!"

After he was hospitalized, my second sister and I prayed for his salvation for two months. I sat by his bed after giving lectures at university. My mother had another stroke and had been hospitalized in a nursing home. My sister, who ministers in a church, shared the gospel and the certainty of pardon while staying the night with him. He finally admitted that he was a sinner and asked for God's forgiveness for the scars he inflicted on the family, especially on mother. And gracefully, he accepted Christ as a savior. A few days later, he passed away as if he had entered into a deep rest, putting down the heavy burden of his life.

After I started believing in God, I prayed for my parents almost every morning. A faithful God unloaded from my shoulder that heavy twenty-year burden of praying. My father used to call me early in the morning to complain about something. I always tried to persuade him that no one is evil toward him, that he should try to love them first. I am not sure whether he listened to me or not, but I am sure that he needed someone to listen to him, whether he was right or wrong.

The difficult family situation affected each family member a lot. My eldest sister had to help out our parents and had to skip a lot of classes. It has been a lifetime of regret for her that she had to sacrifice herself for the family and could not be properly educated. When I was young, she also took care of me. My second sister got a job right after high school taking care of her younger brothers. She sacrificed her education, even marriage, for the family. My brothers could not plan their lives as they wanted due to the difficult family situation, and my third sister also had to take care of father and do house chores after mother had a disc operation.

This difficulty did not stop at my family, but it caused a lot of suffering for my brothers and sisters-in-law. This life's burden left a huge scar on everyone in the family, and the relationship with father was always difficult. But it had some advantages. In order not to repeat this difficult family situation and avoid poverty, my brothers and sisters worked hard for a better future.

Everything worked out together for the good. My brothers and sisters now have their own happy families, and especially our second sister, who became a minister in a church after she met Christ during the difficult moment in her life. God used the family suffering as a tool to make the whole family turn to God.

Now, Mom's condition is deteriorating because of the strokes and Alzheimers. Even now, if I visit her in a nursing home, she recognizes me and smiles at me brightly. I go to her once a week and sing a hymn beside her bed, 'Thou, My Everlasting Portion.'

> *"Thou, my everlasting portion,*
> *More than friend or life to me*
> *All along my pilgrim journey,*
> *Saviour, let me walk with Thee.*
> *Close to Thee, close to Thee,*
> *Close to Thee, close to Thee*
> *All along my pilgrim journey,*
> *Saviour, let me walk with Thee."*

Now she only remembers the phrase 'All along my pilgrim journey, Saviour, let me walk with Thee' of the song that she liked that much.

Then I pray, "Dear Lord, to my beloved mother who is sick in bed alone, please be her friend, be her joy, be everything to her, and put her tears and all sufferings in your wineskin."

Then Mom prays back, worrying about me, "Please Lord, take care of my son."

Watching her, I learn what love is. She worries about me while in such a despairing situation. My heart melts to see her asking about whether I eat well, and why I am coughing.

Jesus said that the kingdom of heaven is like selling all one has to buy hidden treasure and fine pearls. These words give me comfort when I look back on my father and when I watch my mother getting weaker every day. There is a heaven which will offer them the best things, better than anything in this world, more precious than all the wealth, power and glory in this world. Compared to heaven, how worthless all things are! It makes me realize that I am a citizen of the kingdom of God, and my life in this world is being just a holy wayfarer and a faithful steward.

I will not cry now because I know when I face God in heaven, there will be no more tears, no more harm, no more suffering; but there will be only peace and joy. I smile at Mom, and she smiles back. Since God makes us smile, we smile in peace. I am sure God smiles with us. My mom's face, who went through the valley of sufferings and tears with patience and love, is prettier than pearls and the faces of angels.

Epilogue

God does not ask much of us: a thought of Him from time to time, or an act of worship; sometimes to pray for His grace, sometimes to offer up your sufferings, sometimes to thank Him for His favors to you, past and present; and to comfort yourself with thoughts of Him so often as you can. Lift up your heart to Him sometimes when you are at meals or in society; the least little remembrance will always be pleasing to Him. There is no need to cry very loudly, for He is nearer to us than we think.

(Brother Laurence)

It is around 5 am. This is the time that I usually wake up. I meditate on God's words. I pray that God is with me today and that I may live like a child of God. Then I do other things like checking email, reading a book, writing a book or doing research until breakfast. I go to my office walking the same road every day. It is just a five-minute walk. Though this is a road with small bushes, I like this road better than the small alley in Paris that I used to walk, the road in a pretty village in Switzerland, the ancient road in Budapest that I walked once. Even though I walk the same road every day, I pray that tomorrow would be filled with more meaningful things, I would meet better people, and there would be happier things.

My life here is simple. My life would always be the same as a scholar with one hand with the Bible and the other hand with math. But each moment, my soul would be filled with holiness and hope, and I would breathe with a prayer. I want to live my daily life with holy repetition. To fill the present with a beautiful hope is my duty, and that is my formula to live with joy.

C.S. Lewis wrote in his book 'The Screwtape letters,' "The humans live in time but our Enemy destines them to eternity. He, therefore, I believe, wants them to attend chiefly to two things, to eternity itself, and to that point of time which they call the Present. For the Present is the point at which time touches eternity."

Hence, I am faithful to the present, which touches eternity.

My life may look monotonous to people, but to me, it is a creative way containing thousands of colors. That is the way that I chose, and that is the narrow road that I like. I am standing here today as a small and weak man, but as a man supported by the strong Holy Spirit. I do not know where I will be. But I will try to live out my life and in this society in holiness, with the heart of Jesus, and as Jesus did, I will proclaim the power of the gospel to the life of people.

Some composers never discard a piece until it is completed. Once completed, he decides on its publication or not. He says, "Until I do my best to complete it, I will never discard it." I do not know how my life will be until it finishes. If I sweat on it and do my best on it, I will never regret it. I believe God will call such a life a 'masterpiece,' even though it looks shabby.

I always reflect on the life of Abraham. Whenever he wanted to lower the sail of hope and not trust God's promise, Yahweh appeared to remind him of His promise by making him count the sand of the beach and by showing him the countless stars in the sky to light up the flame of his faith. Until he was reborn as the father of faith, he once lied that his wife was his sister to save his life. However, he came to the point that he could dedicate his only son to God, even though his son was born when he was 100, after he had migrated from Haran to Canaan, from Canaan to Egypt, from Egypt to Canaan again, for 25 years.

Since he was a traveler, he did not claim any land or any property. If God told him to leave, he packed his tent to go to the land that God promised.

By this, he must have learned that his everlasting portion is not Canaan, neither Isaac, who will succeed him, but Yahweh himself. That is why he could return his son Isaac, whom he received after twenty-five years of waiting. He knew very well that he could not claim Isaac as his because he would never have had him without God.

Our everlasting portion is God himself in our wayfaring life. I also realize that on my pilgrim journey of life, my everlasting portion, my endless joy, is Yahweh himself.

In front of my office, I can see many trees. Cherry blossoms, red azalea, white peony and yellow bell flowers are in full blossom during the spring. I take a walk when I feel tired of studying. I pray that students passing by may be led to a better life and the truth. I am living as a scholar, a father, a husband, a son, a brother and more importantly as a child of God. I will live my life to the fullest every moment so that my inner being will not wither in the midst of busy life.

Someone said, "I do not pray more than 10 minutes, but I do not stop praying more than 10 minutes either."

I want to be like that. I want to be connected to Him in every part and every moment of my life. As a person called for holiness, as a chosen people, and as a faithful priest, I want to be joyful in God and in his kingdom.

I dedicate this book to those who never give up being in the hands of God, depending on the light from above, on Him who guides us through to the next moment in the bottom of our life, and in the midst of sufferings and despair.

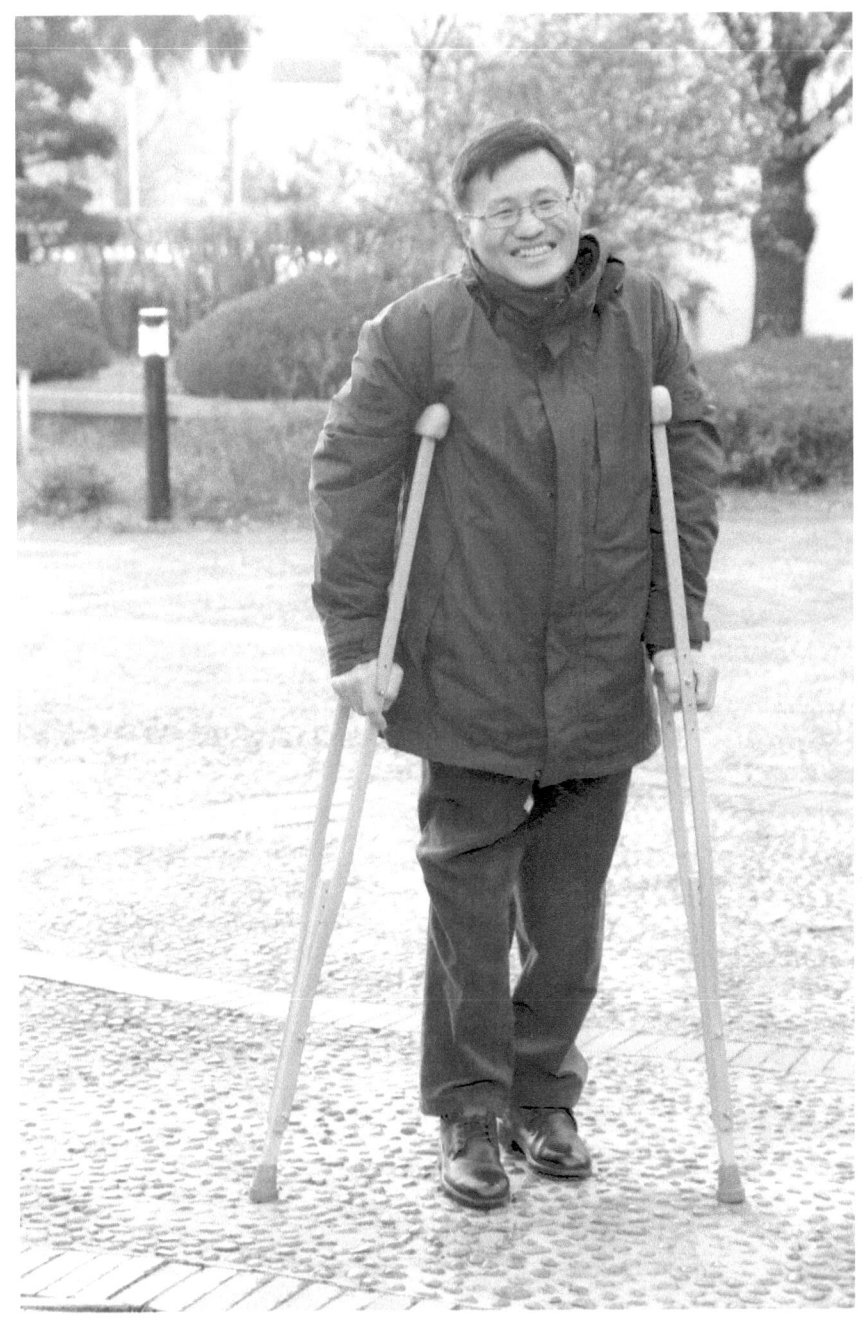